DATE DUE

BRODART, CO.   Cat. No. 23-221-003

Ways of Knowing in Science and Mathematics Series
RICHARD DUSCHL, SERIES EDITOR

Inside
Science Education
Reform

*A History of
Curricular and Policy Change*

J MYRON ATKIN
PAUL BLACK

Teachers College
Columbia University
New York

Published by Teachers College Press, 1234 Amsterdam Avenue, New York, NY 10027

Library of Congress Cataloging-in-Publication Data

Atkin, J Myron.
  Inside science education reform : a history of curricular and policy change / J Myron Atkin, Paul Black.
      p. cm. — (Ways of knowing in science and mathematics series)
Includes bibliographical references and index.
    ISBN 0-8077-4318-6 (pbk. : alk. paper)
   1. Science—Study and teaching—History—20th century. 2. Curriculum change—History—20th century. I. Black, Paul. II. Title. III. Series.
Q181 .A835 2003
507´.1´073—dc21

                                                          2003040194

ISBN 0-8077-4318-6 (paper)

Printed on acid-free paper
Manufactured in the United States of America

10 09 08 07 06 05 04 03   8 7 6 5 4 3 2 1

Contents

Acknowledgments

Many of our intellectual debts to friends and colleagues are incorporated in the stories that constitute the heart of this book. In addition, Mike (J Myron) Atkin would like to thank colleagues and students at the University of Illinois at Urbana-Champaign and at Stanford University—as well as the scores of elementary and secondary school teachers with whom he has worked over several decades—for their friendship, intellectual stimulation, and inspiration. Several funding agencies provided financial assistance for this work, especially the National Science Foundation.

Paul Black would like to thank numerous colleagues at the University of Birmingham, at Chelsea College, and lastly at King's College with whom he has enjoyed, over many years, both stimulus and support. He also acknowledges a debt to many organizations, both national and international, and notably to the Nuffield Foundation, who have given him opportunities and support on numerous occasions.

Major portions of the book were discussed and written at the Rockefeller Foundation's Bellagio Study Center. We are grateful for the collaborative residencies that made it possible for us to work intensively on the project at that remarkable and lovely place. Not least, the Center made it possible for our wives, Ann Atkin and Mary Black, to join us. In addition to familial support, they were invaluable in helping us reconstruct more than half a century of our professional lives.

Introduction

This book, oriented toward both practice and policy, examines many of the successive changes in science education that were initiated from the start of World War II to the beginning of the 21st century. These six decades were particularly eventful: There were new and powerful forces in the development of science education policy. Curriculum was modified frequently—and sometimes radically. New ways of teaching were developed. Patterns of student assessment began to change. There were increased demands on teachers, as well as fresh opportunities.

The main focus of this volume is on the scope, nature, depth, and impact of many of the changes that were attempted. It describes examples of the projects that were devised to improve science education, the curricula produced, the teacher education programs launched, the assessment schemes planned and instituted, and the evaluations of the innovations. The book is not, however, a comprehensive or complete examination of science education during the 60 years. It is more personal. How did the two of us, both of whom were active participants in the events we describe, experience the successive waves of reform? How were our own efforts in science education shaped by these changes? How did we try to influence the course of events in which we were involved, and with what success?

We try to integrate and compare our two perspectives on these developments and our own participation during the period. The professional life of Paul Black took shape in Britain, of Mike Atkin in the United States. Paul started as a physics researcher and gradually reoriented his attention and activities, first toward issues of university-level education in science, then to elementary and secondary schools. Mike started as a high school science teacher, moved to elementary schools, and then shifted to curriculum development, education research, and the evaluation of educational programs. Both of us were active on key national and international committees to advise on science education policy. Both of us conducted research in science education. Both of us spent most of our careers at universities preparing researchers in science education and science teachers.

The notion of a personal perspective on the six decades seemed intuitively appealing to us, but we were fortified in this inclination by growing awareness during recent decades of the opportunities and potential advantages associated with anchoring observations and analysis in personal experience. First-person accounts may not be generalizable in the same sense as some other approaches to understanding; knowledge bred from close encounters and emotional engagement is qualitatively different. But it can have a special kind of depth and integrity because the authors care deeply about the events that they experienced directly and sometimes helped to shape. Not least, writing this book has allowed us to think more carefully not only about the role that we played and about ourselves, but also about the developments that we describe.

Though the personal strand is more intimate, both elements of the book—the broad perspectives on science education during this period and the ones from up close—are detailed and rich in incident. Furthermore, this volume is subjective as well as personal. Because of our interests and predilections, we chose to write about some developments and not others. Because of our intense involvement in many of the activities that are described, we are partial. Because of our own career choices and policy preferences, we gravitated toward topics in which we have, or had, a vested interest. We try to tender these biases to the reader, along with their sources. There are, to be sure, differences between us. They lie mostly in our own professional origins: Paul's as a research physicist, and Mike's as a teacher in elementary and secondary schools. The differences are neither hidden nor exaggerated.

What happened during those 60 years, then? What were the influential forces? What was accomplished? What seemed (and seems) problematic? What are the continuing challenges? World War II played a powerful role in ushering in an era of deep and rapid transformation of science education, one somewhat surprisingly that is still accelerating. Scientific research came to be seen as a key element of national defense during the war years, and improved technical education of the nation's population was seen as essential for military preparedness. An unusually large number of influential, research-oriented, university-based scientists who had spent World War II designing weaponry turned their attention to education improvement. Private foundations provided initial support. Later the government joined in and dominated the effort. The World War II scientists, joined gradually by others at universities, provided both the impetus and the initial conceptual leadership.

By the late 1970s, the science professors' priorities and influence began to wane. Public attention never strayed far from science education, but the reasons for anxiety about the quality of science education expanded: improve the economy, prepare people for employment, protect the environment, help people use new technologies, equip all citizens—scientists and non-scientists alike—to make intelligent decisions as voters about technically based public policy. With the proliferation of the goals for science education, new stakeholders became more active and prominent—and politicians, parents, teachers, and the press more assertive. The personal and social uses of science (and technology) became more pronounced in some of the new curriculum programs, in addition to (and sometimes instead of) the more basic-research interests of university-based scientists.

The story presented here is essentially thematic and chronological. We examine such matters as the shifting aspirations for the schools, the forces for change in science education, the periodic reconceptualization of educational goals, the evolving conceptions of what it takes to actually modify educational practices, the curriculum and teacher education innovations, the changing roles of teachers, the problematic features of our methods of assessing students, and the shifting demands of public accountability.

Education policy inevitably plays out against a background of broader concerns: economic conditions in a given period, demographic shifts, political pressures, public expectations, and much more. Therefore other school subjects can be presumed to be changing in similar ways. Accountability pressures, for example, apply across the curriculum and have consequences in testing programs in almost all fields. So does the standards movement. So does the attractiveness of teaching as a profession in a given decade. While our story is about science education only, and the examples center exclusively on this subject, the broader educational, social, and political scene influences the entire education enterprise.

What really counts in education is what happens when teachers and students meet. The wisdom of any decision about education is best judged on the basis of whether or not it raises the quality of those interactions. This book aims to influence the decisions that are made by policymakers and the general public with respect to two particular factors that affect classroom life: teachers and research. The former is central, but often problematic; the latter is peripheral, and usually problematic.

The initial chapters outline how the aims of science education (Chapter 1) and the accompanying curriculum (Chapter 2) provide much of the context for what plays out in the classroom among students and between students and the teacher. We go on to examine some issues associated with the somewhat permeable boundaries of science education itself (Chapter 3), the association between teaching and learning (Chapter 4), and the central and expanding place of assessment in connecting the two

(Chapter 5). We then turn to research in science education (Chapter 6) and the teachers themselves (Chapter 7), followed by a short conclusion (Chapter 8) about how wiser policy with regard to both can improve the quality of science education.

1

Aims and Politics of Science Education

Aims for education in all countries are derived from the society at large. It is a truism that schools are expected by the public to reflect and transmit the values, wisdom, and views of history that prevail in any nation at a given time. Increasingly, however, schools are being asked to be an instrument in addressing current national problems. In a growing number of countries, the education system is being placed at or near the front line in attacking pervasive and serious challenges such as a marked decline in international economic competitiveness, a perceived weakening of military power, or rising unemployment. In the United States about 50 years ago, the schools were designated as the primary social institution for combating the country's most deep-rooted long-standing and serious domestic problem: race relations. The Supreme Court in 1954 concluded that schools should play the major role in eradicating racial isolation. As segregated schools are inherently unequal, it is intolerable that they continue to exist, said the justices. The direct implications for the schools were immediate and monumental, more so than for any other American institution.

This view of the public schools as a policy instrument to effect major changes originated in the 19th century. A polyglot population from dozens of countries was converging on a new nation. What did the many immigrants from different places, embracing different religions, have in common? What *might* they have? In short, what does it mean to be an American? In the soul searching for a place and method to build a shared heritage and sense of values, the "common" schools were created. The free and public schools became a sort of secular church, an institution that would welcome and integrate people of different national lineages and religions and serve as an instrument for forging a new sense of nationhood. It

1

is perhaps this cultural memory that leads Americans to see the schools today as a vehicle for promoting change as well as reflecting it. Whether or not the schools can serve such a purpose is open to debate, but the fact that the citizenry continues to try is not.

A similar impetus and result can be seen in the growth of public schooling in Britain in the 1800s. One main motivation was the fear of the social unrest that might follow if the underprivileged and uneducated working classes in the burgeoning industrial cities were to have no stake in the future prosperity of the country. The other was that to give them that stake would also meet the need for a more literate and numerate workforce.

While changes in science education are seldom as fraught with consequences as serious as some of the examples above, there are clear echoes of such thinking in the stories that fill this chapter. One reason is that in the United States as in Britain, with the change from a rural and craft economy to an industrial and technologically complex one, improved scientific and technical education is seen increasingly as the key to national progress in dozens of areas. The public demands changes in science education when it is disturbed by a drop in national productivity, or an increased reliance on technically trained workers from abroad, or a decline in the ability of a region to maintain its population base. While there is often consensus about the problem, however, there is usually little agreement about specific ways to address it. Parties with different interests and stakes in an issue can embrace the same general goals, yet suggest or produce different responses, sometimes with considerable acrimony. People might agree that more and better science should be taught in American schools to prepare more people for careers in an increasingly technological society, for example, but there are usually conflicting views about just what that science should be. We try to make such distinctions between aims and suggested solutions (and among the contending parties) clear in the episodes that follow.

MIKE'S STORIES

An Applications-Driven Curriculum

Science has never been a major subject in American schools for children from 5 to 12. While I remember lessons in history, geography, arithmetic, spelling, and art, I recall little that was labeled "science" during my attendance at a public elementary school in Brooklyn, New York, in the 1930s. An aquarium was sometimes positioned near the classroom window. I looked at pictures in textbooks about animal adaptations to seasonal change and remember the teacher talking about hibernation and protective coloration. However, I have no recollection of specific lessons that I associated with science during all of my attendance in grades kindergarten through six.

Seventh grade (in the same school) was different. A specially designated teacher now taught science as a defined subject on a regular basis twice a week. The emphasis in this new subject was unequivocally on the *uses* of science. Textbooks had titles that emphasized science in daily life or everyday problems in science. There were sessions in class that taught me how to wire flashlight bulbs to dry-cell batteries in series and in parallel. The message was that parallel circuitry was employed in homes, so that each appliance had full voltage, and all the lights did not go out when one was turned off. I built (and blew) fuses I had constructed from the metal foil in chewing gum wrappers. Central heating was relatively new, and we built a model of a hot water heating system to learn how it functioned. This particular construction activity was followed by the teacher's demonstration of convection currents in water—and, when we got to hot-air heating systems, in air.

When I started graduate school at New York University in 1947, I learned that this focus on applications of science had not always been the foundation of the science curriculum. It had originated at Columbia University's Teachers College only about a decade before I entered elementary school, and gained momentum with publication of the 31st Yearbook of the National Society for the Study of Education (NSSE), *A Program for Teaching Science* (1932). As for all the NSSE yearbooks before and since, experts in the field had been assembled, chaired in this case by S. Ralph Powers of Teachers College. They endorsed and amplified the most important trends they saw developing, especially those they wished to promote. The early decades of the century had been marked by increasing public awareness of the impact of scientific advance on people and society. Serious childhood diseases such as diphtheria were being prevented by new immunizations. Daily life was being altered significantly by the introduction of labor-saving devices, like refrigerators to replace iceboxes.

I must have been eight or nine years old in the mid-1930s when a natural-gas refrigerator was installed in our Brooklyn apartment; it was a mystery to me how a flame could be used to keep food cold. My mother talked of the "injections" to ward off diseases that my younger brother was able to receive and that were not available when I was an infant only six years earlier. The gasoline engine had altered the face of the nation; paved roads and automobiles were virtually everywhere (even on Prospect Place, where they began to interfere with stickball and other street games.) More dramatically, by the 1920s a person who could pay the price was able to board an airplane in New York and arrive in Los Angeles a little more than 24 hours later. All of this, and much more, was a clear sign that science and engineering had impressive consequences for human beings. The purpose of science teaching turned toward helping students understand how principles of science were making their lives safer and more productive. So we learned about four-stroke-cycle gasoline engines, principles of refrigeration, and Bernoulli's Principle.

Science to Fit the Times

I learned later that an emphasis on applications represented a profound shift away from an earlier approach to the teaching of science that was popular in the first decade of the 20th century. It was called Nature Study and was created to address what was seen as a serious social problem: urbanization. People were leaving rural areas in great numbers to move to the rapidly expanding cities. The character of the United States and the identity of its people had been shaped in a huge land of farms and small towns. The culture of the nation was closely associated with the country life. Muckrakers like Lincoln Steffens and Upton Sinclair wrote graphically about the evils of the city. Not for the first time, or the last, a school-based response was created to address a serious social problem. In this case the goal, literally, was to use school science to keep people down on the farm.

With leadership from Cornell University in New York—actually its College of Agriculture—the new subject was invented and introduced to present content designed to glorify the rural life. Its explicit aim was to teach children to love nature. The reasoning was that if students came to develop an emotional attachment to the countryside, the rate of urbanization would be reduced. To achieve this end, biological topics were emphasized more than those in the physical sciences. And for the purpose of increasing psychological identification with objects and organisms in nature, a strong anthropomorphic flavor was introduced into instructional materials for children. Books were published in which birds talked with trees as well as with their own offspring. Insects spoke to one another. Illustrations of forests took on human form, with faces on tree trunks and branches that looked like arms. Mature compound flowers gave lectures to flower buds.

In keeping with a science framework, almost all this talk was about their respective parts. Thus, the mature flower spoke to the flower bud of the stamens and pistils the bud would develop as it grew older. In the process of such teaching, a great deal of technical botany and zoology became part of the curriculum, but always for the primary purpose of assisting students to identify with nature in such as way as to develop a close attachment. Even the lesser amount of physical science took on human characteristics. Electrons, for example, soon sprouted legs and were running through wires to help children understand about current flow.

The movement emanating from Cornell resulted in creation of a full-sized Department of Education within the College of Agriculture for the purpose of changing science teaching in the schools. (The Education Department persists in Agriculture to this day, though not for the purpose of promulgating Nature Study.) Outstanding botanists and entomologists at the university with national reputations contributed to the new Nature Study curriculum. Furthermore, in one of the most ambitious efforts at curriculum "dissemination" up to that time, the *Cornell Rural School Leaflets* were published, then distributed widely, influentially, and expensively in New York State and elsewhere. They continued to be published right up to the 1970s.

Aims for teaching science in schools, I learned, were malleable—and contested. When priorities began to shift toward applications of science in daily life and away from Nature Study, there was serious competition, even conflict, between the younger group at Columbia University's Teachers College and those at Cornell, with both vying for the hearts and minds of teachers, children, and the public at large. The friction between Cornell and Columbia persisted at least until my beginning graduate school years, when my science education professors were still citing the 31st NSSE Yearbook for its departure from Nature Study, as well as for its advocacy of an applications-based curriculum.

It may be noteworthy that my own applications-driven science education at the secondary-school level took place in a special public high school in New York City, Stuyvesant, that was created specifically to cater to boys who were thought to have special science and/or mathematics potential. Many could be expected to develop careers in science, and did. Yet the focus still was on applications. In biology, for example, conservation was a dominant theme. The country was traumatized in the 1930s by dust storms and floods in the Midwest that aggravated both the economic and psychological depressions. People were impoverished and hungry. Employment prospects were bleak for many, resulting in huge migrations from Middle America to the West, particularly California. As a consequence of some of these conditions, biology texts went into considerable detail about erosion of soil by wind and water and how to mitigate it. They also stressed practices to promote good health, including immunization procedures, public sanitation, and desirable nutritional practices. As part of the latter, the students were taught not only about the benefits of a balanced diet but also, with value for a dollar a Depression-era priority, about the nutritional features of a long list of inexpensive foods. In my first teaching position in

1948, in a small private high school on 82nd Street in Manhattan, the biology textbook from which I taught devoted several chapters to detailed explanations of contour plowing, crop rotation, and the planting of trees to blunt the force of prairie winds.

Making Students Better Thinkers

The 46th Yearbook of the NSSE, *Science Education in American Schools,* turned out to be another key document in my graduate education (National Society for the Study of Education, 1947). The 46th Yearbook embraced the science-in-daily-life themes of the 31st Yearbook 15 years earlier with respect to selection of content to be conveyed, but it added a new objective: teaching problem solving and the scientific method. This conception of teaching and learning was influenced heavily by the writings of John Dewey, particularly his *How We Think* (1910). Dewey, like almost everyone, was impressed both by scientific achievement and by the kinds of thought processes that made it possible. He believed passionately in bringing both to the classroom.

As a Ph.D. student (part-time) in the late 1940s and early 1950s, I was much influenced by Dewey, as my professors had been. The process of thinking, Dewey posited, begins in a problematic situation. A problem doesn't become one in the Deweyan sense, however, until the situation itself is problematized (Dewey, 1938). By that he meant that the learner must begin to imagine a way to resolve the matter before problem solving actually can begin. His 1910 formulation described scientific methods as including elements like identifying and defining the problem, collecting data, formulating a hypothesis, testing a hypothesis, drawing a conclusion, and applying the conclusion in new situations in which similar factors were operating. Picking up research priorities of the time, this aspect of science education formed part of the conceptual basis for my own doctoral dissertation.

It was no surprise to me or my advisors when my research suggested that those students who had greater influence in shaping the problems they investigated were more creative in formulating hypotheses and more systematic and probing in testing them (Atkin, 1958). Thus I became sensitized to the possible relationship between a psychological construct (the nature of scientific thinking, in this case) and a pedagogical approach (engaging students as agents in their own learning). I did not apprehend until many years later the possibility that specific pedagogies could be consistent with several different theories and therefore not necessarily dependent on any one of them.

Actually, I had become aware of the notion of devising a science curriculum for the primary purpose of improving the mind when I learned about the Object Teaching movement of the late 1800s, a teaching approach that was popular before Nature Study. Faculty psychology was the dominant psychological theory at the time. It postulated that the mind is constituted of many different "faculties," such as observation, memorization, generalization, and reasoning. A primary function of education was to develop them. Object Teaching, invented in England but widely adopted in the United States, consisted of bringing certain objects to class: india rubber, a bird's beak, an acorn, among hundreds of others. Young children up to about age 11, not yet possessing the faculties of generalization and reasoning, according to the theory, could nevertheless develop those of observation and memorization.

It is clear enough how to give children practice in memorization and make assessments of how much they have learned. But what about observation? The chosen method was to see how discriminating the student could become at ascribing a range of adjectives to the objects brought to class. A widely used manual for teachers at the time (Sheldon, 1872) listed those that were to be used accurately and memorized by children from ages 8 to 11. Not atypical were words such as *argillaceous, oleaginous, vitrifiable, chalybeate*, and *ductile*.

"Integrating" the Science Curriculum as a New Goal

In 1950, I moved from high school teaching in New York City to elementary school science teaching in Great Neck, a suburban community just over the city boundary. By then my interest in how children think about science had gelled. It seemed to me that younger children were more spontaneous in their actions and more transparent in their thoughts than older students. So I took advantage of the opportunity to work with them full-time.

The general aims for science education were similar in Great Neck to what I had seen at the high school level. I was expected to focus on topics that the students were familiar with in their everyday lives and, at the same time, stress problem-solving activities in my pedagogical approach. My specific role was that of a resource person to the 25 regular classroom teachers in the kindergarten-to-grade-6 school to which I was assigned. The general philosophy was that the day-to-day classroom teacher, as the person who knew the students best, would design the entire curriculum. She might need help with science, however, because elementary school teachers generally do not receive much preparation in the subject.

My work with Marion Billhardt, a third-grade teacher, illustrates how I was expected to assist teachers. Mrs. Billhardt told me one day in March that her students had become quite concerned about the fact that the local authorities had decided to close the nearby bathing beach to swimmers during the coming summer. It was too polluted. She believed that this situation had potential for the students to learn about pollution and its causes, and also about how the community might be mobilized to do something about it.

Most of the speculation about the cause of the problem centered on a particular sewage disposal plant on the north shore of Long Island Sound that probably was releasing inadequately treated waste. She and I worked together to plan a series of activities for the students. They would find out where bacteria are found. They would find out what they need in order to multiply and how rapidly they would do so. They would experiment with antiseptics to inhibit their growth.

Mrs. Billhardt believed that students should understand how the different academic subjects relate to one another, how they might be "integrated" in the pursuit of studies in the real world. So she also introduced the concept of a geometric progression in estimating how long it would take for a small number of bacteria to grow to billions. She arranged for the class to visit a sewage treatment plant to learn how effluents are made less toxic. She also made them aware that a bill had been introduced in the state legislature by Assemblyman Ostertag to build a new disposal plant on the north shore. Presumably, this step would reduce pollution enough in Long Island Sound to minimize the possibility of needing to close their bathing beach in the future. Mrs. Billhardt used the prospect of legislation on the subject to teach the students something about how the bicameral New York state legislature operates. The students decided, with their teacher's encouragement, to write letters urging passage of the proposed law to create the new facility. This led to lessons on letter writing. Every student in the class wrote one. They then examined the letters, established criteria for a high-quality letter, and then chose three to send to the local weekly newspaper. In a cover letter to the editor, the children expressed the hope that one of the letters would be printed. All three were published. They also received a letter of appreciation from Assemblyman Ostertag.

Work like this with Mrs. Billhardt and her third graders provided a concreteness to the ideas of John Dewey and the NSSE Yearbooks. In the hands of teachers like her, students were engaged seriously in their schoolwork and seemed to be learning a great deal. It solidified my own emerging convictions about the most desirable types of science education. I also began to understand how much more skill was entailed in planning a curriculum of this type: It was infinitely more demanding of teachers than the conventional textbook-oriented courses, and required teachers of special commitment and ability.

The Postwar Reforms and New Goals for Science:
Science for Science's Sake

In 1955, after five years of teaching in Great Neck and in the throes of completing my Ph.D., I moved to the University of Illinois. The move coincided almost exactly with the start of yet another curriculum movement, one in which outstanding members of the academic community were turning their attention to reformulating the aims and methods of science and mathematics education in elementary and secondary schools. Importantly for me, this science and mathematics curriculum reform movement had originated at the University of Illinois just a few years before I got there. Max Beberman, a mathematics teacher at the university's laboratory school and a professor of education, and Herbert Vaughn, a mathematics professor, had created the University of Illinois Committee on School Mathematics (UICSM). The general stance of the new project was that existing school mathematics was centered primarily on everyday applications (discount and compound interest problems and balancing checkbooks, for example) and that the curriculum, in fact, contained no mathematics invented since the 17th century. The goal of UICSM was to align school mathematics more closely to the kinds of mathematics that contemporary research-level mathematicians found interesting.

A new high school course was created that emphasized such topics as set and number theory. Students were asked to perform calculations in number systems other than base 10, for example. Mathematical ideas were taught for their own sake, not for their utility; the course eschewed applications in favor of deeper mathematical ideas. Carnegie Corporation, a private foundation, funded the UICSM project in 1952, which helped greatly to accord it professional and public visibility. UICSM was the first effort in the United States to exemplify a process by which central responsibility for identifying important content for school-age students was assigned primarily to scholars in the various disciplines who are at the frontiers of research. By this reasoning, only such scholars know enough about the subject to decide what's worth teaching. This emphasis was later extended to encompass not only the key concepts within the disciplines, but also how leading scientists think about their disciplinary worlds, that is, the styles of thought that characterize their respective fields.

The National Science Foundation

By 1956, the orientation exemplified by UICSM had spread to science, starting with physics. The Physical Sciences Study Committee (PSSC), a consortium of researchers from MIT and Harvard and some industrial scientists in the Cambridge, Massachusetts, area led by MIT professor of physics Jerrold Zacharias, was created to develop an analogous course. It soon garnered financial support from the National Science Foundation (NSF), the first curriculum development project to do so. The new science education reform movement was launched. It was to reverberate around the world.

It would be difficult to overestimate the importance of the prestige and sheer drive of some of the scientists in the late 1950s and early 1960s who became involved in primary and secondary education. Many of them had been involved deeply in large and ambitious World War II projects, such as those at the Radiation Lab at MIT that helped to develop radar, and the Manhattan Project that designed and built the atomic bomb. Scientists involved in such efforts, like Zacharias, were disproportionately involved in the new curriculum work. They had learned that exceptional talent and extensive resources could accomplish monumental tasks. Having designed radar and built the bomb, they were not in awe of the challenge to reinvent American education.

This sense of the possible was contagious. It was also uplifting for science teachers like me. Some of the nation's most respected and famous scientists, people who had played key roles in helping the United States and its allies win a world war, were saying that our work in the classroom was absolutely critical to the country's future. It made us teachers feel that we counted, that we were being enlisted for a new front line to improve the country. Even more than that, though, the career to which we had committed ourselves was not only socially valued, it was intellectually challenging. Why else would such brilliant people be deeply involved?

The NSF did not come to the decision to enter the curriculum development field lightly or quickly. Moving into the territory of *what* to teach was a difficult matter politically because the U.S. Constitution leaves matters of education to the individual states. There was much counsel within the National Science Board, the policymaking group for NSF, to be cautious. The UICSM precedent that had been launched with funding from a private philanthropic foundation was emboldening, however. The NSF took the plunge. (The political backlash for entering the curriculum field did not come until the mid-1970s and is described in the chapter on assessment and evaluation.)

By the late 1950s, the foundation had provided support to several additional curriculum efforts in addition to PSSC: the School Mathematics Study Group, led by Ed Begle, who moved from Yale to Stanford; the ChemStudy program at the University of California at Berkeley; the Chemical Bond program in Indiana; the Biological Sciences Curriculum Study in Colorado; the Earth Sciences Curriculum Project in Colorado; and others. All of them advanced the core assumption of UICSM and PSSC: Top-level academic scientists and mathematicians are the people to determine the aims and content of courses in these fields for elementary and secondary schools. There were also NSF-supported teacher institutes by the scores (later to expand to the hundreds) in colleges and universities all over the country. Most of them began to promote the NSF-supported curriculum projects.

Changes in Elementary School Science

In 1958, caught up in the developing momentum for changes in the curriculum to reflect the views of academic scientists, I advanced the proposition that the elementary school curriculum should be changed in a similar fashion. Curriculum at that level, too, should be determined by professors with the deepest grasp of the subject. Looking back, I am dismayed by my own opportunism. In what seems now like a cavalier disregard of both my experience in Great Neck and my ideological predilections, I forged a partnership with Stanley Wyatt, an Illinois professor of astronomy. Wyatt was well known on campus for his interest in teaching and was quite amenable to working with students below the college level. He was also a friend. So we examined our common interests and decided to approach the National Science Foundation.

We were delighted to learn that the staff at the NSF also wanted to move into elementary school science with programs analogous to those it had initiated at the high school level. There were serious difficulties, however. James Conant, chemist and former president of Harvard University, was chairman at the time of the National Science Board, the NSF governing body, and he opposed the move for NSF to become involved in science education improvement below the high school level. He was also the person on the board most knowledgeable about and involved in education, having been the leading figure in establishing a new undergraduate science sequence for non-science majors at Harvard and in leading a highly visible study of American secondary education.

For Conant, it was a matter of scale, not fundamental principle. He reasoned that NSF's programs had a realistic chance of reaching a large percentage of the 30,000 to 40,000 teachers of mathematics and science in the country in 1958 in a reasonable number of years. New courses could be developed and the institute program expanded. But how could the foundation make a dent in an elementary school teacher cohort of about a million? Furthermore, secondary school teachers were a fairly stable group; they tended to remain in teaching for their entire careers. Not so for elementary school teachers. Chemist Conant noted that this largely female group had a half-life of about three years. At the time, it was not uncommon for women to enter teaching until they started to raise a family, and then leave. The clinching argument for caution, at least for a year or two, was that elementary school teachers, unlike those in secondary school, not only had responsibility for teaching science but all other subjects as well.

Since there was support within the NSF staff for a move to elementary schools, Wyatt and I were encouraged to devise a modest approach the foundation might take to test the elementary school waters. After extended discussion, the board agreed to experiment. For the summer of 1959, a grant was awarded to the University of Illinois for an experimental summer institute that Wyatt and I co-directed for *leadership* figures in elementary school science. The fact that a presumably more permanent group of people than regular classroom teachers was the target, and that each of them, in turn, reached other teachers, addressed Conant's objections well enough for NSF to proceed. The nature of the leadership roles of potential participants was to be described in their applications. Mostly they were principals or science supervisors. At the institute, the group would study ecology and astronomy. Since the effort was experimental, a supplementary grant was awarded that enabled me to travel to the school districts of each of the 45 participants to follow up and evaluate the influence of the summer program on their work in their respective districts.

Meanwhile, to further counter Conant's reservations, the American Association for the Advancement of Science (AAAS) was given a grant by the NSF to ascertain the feasibility of moving into the elementary school field. Three invitational conferences were held around the country involving outstanding scientists and educators who deliberated about pros and cons. The result was a strong recommendation about the importance of teaching science and mathematics to young children.

The report was published in its entirety in the AAAS's widely read and respected journal, *Science*. The board gave its approval for further efforts at the elementary school level. With Wyatt and me as co-directors, Illinois was awarded a "course content improvement" grant to develop a curriculum in astronomy for students aged 11 to 14. I had learned a lesson about science education politics: To forge a consensus around a contested policy option, convene mostly like-minded experts with impressive credentials to develop position papers and recommendations.

Goals of Science Education in Other Countries

Soon after the conclusion of the astronomy project in 1966 (which is described in greater detail in the next chapter), I was invited to become associate dean for research at the College of Education at the University of Illinois, then dean two years later. The detour into university administration was to last for 20 years, the last seven at Stanford.

On leaving the Stanford education deanship in 1986, I had the chance, on a year's leave, to serve temporarily as "senior advisor" for education at the National Science Foundation. It was a happy and welcome opportunity. From a Washington vantage point, I was in a position to begin to catch up with what was going on in science education around the country, and possibly to even make a contribution to the development of new NSF initiatives in the field (Atkin, 1988).

On returning to Stanford, I was asked by the president of Carnegie Corporation to undertake an evaluation of Carnegie-supported projects that were designed to foster collaboration between schools and "science-rich" institutions (science-based industries, universities, science museums, the military, government laboratories) to improve science education. The evaluation provided yet another crash course on some recent developments in science education by allowing me to visit several dozen schools and talk with school administrators, scientists, and teachers in virtually every region of the country (Atkin & Atkin, 1989).

In about 1990, I learned that the Organization for Economic Cooperation and Development (OECD) in Paris was contemplating a major project to examine innovations in science, mathematics, and technology education. Staff of the OECD's Center for Educational Research and Innovation were trying to figure out how to collect information about new developments that were arising in the member countries. All 25 members of the organization were trying to improve their science and mathematics programs, but there had been no systematic attempt to monitor or analyze what was happening. I had done some work with the OECD in the early 1970s on school improvement, and was invited to become involved in the project. Shortly afterward, Paul Black was invited to join me as co-chair of the steering committee for the entire initiative, which is how we first met. The project was to last for about seven years.

One aspect of the OECD project, in particular, relates to the matter of aims for science education and my own evolving viewpoint. As I worked at the NSF and studied the interinstitutional collaborative efforts supported by Carnegie Corporation, I started to rediscover my old attraction for a Dewey-oriented community-directed socially relevant kind of science education. I was impressed that schools working with local science-based industries were able to help students understand how science connects to concerns in the community and to their own lives. The alliances that Carnegie supported expanded students' horizons and blurred the distinction between school and the world outside—as Mrs. Billhardt had done. I began at the NSF even to see the foundation incorporate engineering research as a full partner with research in the long-established science disciplines.

The OECD project, as it gradually evolved, helped me to learn that the trends in the United States toward more practical and socially relevant work for students were evident by the 1990s in many countries. In Japan, for example, a new curriculum had just been promulgated for elementary school children replacing the subject called "Science" with "Environmental and Life Sciences." The idea was bred of several Japanese concerns: They saw their students as passive and wanted them more involved in initiating and conducting investigations. They saw their children as less creative than others (particularly those in the United States) and wanted them to be involved in genuine community-based problem-solving activity. They were concerned as a nation about environmental degradation and wanted to sensitize school-age children to the dangers.

When I observed a class in a Yokohama City classroom in connection with the OECD work, the 12-year-old students were just embarking on a study of the effects of acid rain. The teacher introduced what would turn out to be a six-week unit by showing videotape he had prepared that provided evidence of deterioration of the concrete on nearby bridges and buildings. The children murmured their surprise and concern when they realized that the video was taken in their own neighborhood. The class then planned a canvas of the community to find other examples of structural damage. Afterward, they learned about the causes of acid rain, how it acts on building materials and humans, where it is produced, how it spreads, and what might be done both to reduce it and mitigate the effects.

In Scotland, technology was introduced into the curriculum to emphasize practical work. In Holland, it became a separate subject for all students, not solely those in vocational education programs. It was becoming part of the curriculum in new curriculum frameworks and courses of study in Ontario, Canada, and Tasmania, Australia. The study would reveal, in fact, that an emphasis on the practical, a 1990s version of science in daily life, was one of the clearest curriculum trends among the OECD countries that participated. A closely related finding was that integrated science was replacing courses in the separate science disciplines: in Spain, Ontario, California, and Germany, for example. (The matter of connections among the separate school subjects is examined in Chapter 3.) And by this time, practical reasoning as a key element of human thought, neglected both in the curriculum and in teacher education, began to move toward the center of my own theoretical interests, a point to which we will return in the chapters on research and teachers.

"Inquiry" as an Emerging Aim of Science Education

As the 20th century drew to a close, an additional aim for science education gained new prominence: inquiry. The National Academy of Sciences is the country's most prestigious scientific organization. It was created in the

Lincoln administration both to recognize outstanding scientific achievement and to advise government about science policy. This organization, with its operating arm, the National Research Council, was designated to develop national standards for science education. Financial support was provided by several governmental and private agencies, but primarily from the National Science Foundation. The resulting effort, the *National Science Education Standards* (National Research Council, 1996) was intended as an inspiration and guide for state and local education authorities. The document is fashioned to identify inquiry as the central theme in providing coherence for standards that are proffered for teaching, professional development, assessment, and content. In fact, inquiry is the first of the science *content* standards.

The provenance of this goal for science education dates back at least to Object Teaching. The improvement of students' abilities to reason scientifically has often been an aim of the curriculum. Dewey highlighted it. It was a popular research focus when I undertook my Ph.D. research. The PSSC course begins with consideration of the nature of light: Is it wavelike or particlelike? The topic is examined at length, mostly to help students understand how scientists think about such matters.

Many of the scientists in the MIT group associated with PSSC had turned their efforts to improvement of science at the elementary school level and were especially committed to the idea of students becoming heavily involved in first hand investigation of the world around them. They developed instructional approaches in which the opportunity to explore and experiment—with batteries and bulbs, with mealworms, with pendulums—were at the heart of the program.

These developments took shape against a background in which there was much talk about "discovery" learning, essentially a point of view that stressed the importance of students engaging in activities in which they themselves would develop important concepts of science through independent investigation. So it was not altogether surprising that the National Academy of Sciences' initiative to develop standards for use in the entire country accorded attention to matters of scientific ways of knowing. What was surprising was that the document placed inquiry as an integral element of content, thus fusing the traditional separation between what is be learned and how one goes about learning it.

PAUL'S STORIES

Just Liking It

Physics was my favourite subject at secondary school, but all pleasures at school were overshadowed as I followed the progress of World War II.

There was a morbid fascination but also fear. I recall seeing the glow on the horizon from the burning of the city of Liverpool, 20 miles away, after an air raid, and also feeling the impact as two bombs fell on the small seaside town where I lived. I was quite unaware that first the physicists, with their radar, and later the mathematicians and other academics, breaking the secret communication codes of the enemy, were tilting the balance of the war.

The science that I was taught was mainly "pure"—applications were extras, added to the menu for interest or as examples, but not in the foreground. In my post-age-16 studies I studied only three subjects—physics, mathematics, and geography. Only in geography did the teacher break out of the schoolbound perspective. The day the class spent in the hills of Snowdonia was a high point amongst several expeditions. The differences between V-shaped and U-shaped valleys, the drumlins, the tree line, and many other features brought physical geography alive. When it came to plotting the paths of railway lines, I came to understand the need to minimize gradients and to strike a balance between the costs of cuttings and embankments and the costs of the alternative detours to follow level ground. Here was a contrast with the physics and mathematics, but not one that gave rise to second thoughts about my priorities. Insofar as I thought of my aim, I took for granted that they were simple—to achieve the highest possible grades in the external examinations, and to pursue the subject that I liked best.

Physics for Its Own Sake

The purity of physics and mathematics was maintained when I entered a physics degree course at Manchester University in 1947. The work lived up to its promise of rewarding intellectual challenge. A second-year essay assignment on the electron microscope and a final-year project on Fourier analysis of waveforms opened wider perspectives, but these were small beer compared with hearing famous physicists lecture on the origin of cosmic rays or on the newly growing subject of radio astronomy. The genesis of the latter research in the wartime development of radar and a lecture on how operational research had been a key part of wartime strategy were signs that in the aftermath of World War II, we could be confident that physics was important to our society, and had indeed helped to save it.

After graduating in 1950, I was able to gain entry to the Cavendish Laboratory in Cambridge. There I worked for six years of almost full-time research, years that developed and deepened my commitment to science as intellectual endeavour. I was only dimly aware that my research, on the crystallography of intermetallic compounds, was funded by government and industry in the belief that it would lead to better alloys. With others in the laboratory making steady progress in unraveling the structure of proteins, and Crick and Watson two floors below working out the double helix of DNA, we all shared the excitement of discovering new secrets of nature. Furthermore, the belief that this knowledge must also be of eventual benefit to all was enough to justify one's existence.

When in 1956 I moved from Cambridge to my first permanent lectureship post in the physics department at the University of Birmingham, my research interests remained pure and, from time to time, compelling. The effects on my later career of devoting about half of my time, for about 25 years, on research were of two kinds. The minor effect was on credibility: When a senior physics professor had to introduce me to give an invited lecture on the teaching of physics, he remarked that I was the one professor of education whom physicists could trust, because I was a real physicist.

The major effect was on my view of science. I had experienced the excitement of searching for a model that gave the best fit to one's data, and I could not forget the tension when, working late at night, I saw the record of a feeble beam of scattered radiation slowly accumulate to the point where I could see whether the experiment, which had taken weeks to prepare, would or would not show that our theoretical prediction matched reality. The sense of interrogating reality was clear and strong. When, in later years, I had to listen to those who argued that the results of science were no more than a social construction, my irritation was tempered with sadness—that they had not experienced the tension, the failures, and the successes. One question that followed was whether this flavour of *doing* science could be conveyed in and through science education.

Taking Aims Seriously

Teaching, through tutorials to undergraduates, was a small part of my Cambridge life, one that a junior researcher just took on, with no training and no briefing on the structure and aims of the undergraduate courses. What had to be done was not a problem: You helped the students with the sheets of problems that their lecturers had handed out, and you tried to help with any difficulties in understanding their lectures that they chose to raise. I had no sense of wider aims, for example, helping the students to become better able to manage their own learning.

With my move to Birmingham I began to take on substantial teaching responsibilities. Aims were taken to be so self-evident that they were never made explicit. Unease about this was provoked by the results from a "general" paper set as a component of the final degree examinations, which tested students not on any particular course, but on general ability as physicists. Results were always disappointing. A notable example was a question about cities: The problem posed was that as the size of a city increases, the proportion of its surface area devoted to roads has to increase. Students were asked to invent a simple algebraic model to represent this situation, and then to speculate about how it might lead to a figure for the maximum feasible size for a city. Hardly any student could make a credible attempt, even those who were about to gain first-class physics degrees. Staff argument raged—was this a fair question; was it applied mathematics, not physics; what had we done to render first-class minds so incapable of tackling such a straightforward problem; where now stood the arguments for a physics degree as training for the mind? For the aim involved here, as for several others latent in this general paper, there had been no explicit formulation, let alone any debate or agreement. The assumption that students would achieve such general aims *en passant* without need for explicit teaching turned out to be unjustified.

One of the obstacles to serious debate about statements of aims was the view amongst my fellow physicists that such statements were merely cosmetic, and that everyone knew, pragmatically, what was good physics. To attempt serious debate about such statements was to risk entrapment in the swamps of educational theory, where ideas would be drowned and nothing useful could emerge. One reason for such skepticism was that we lacked good models of meaningful and useful debates. An American visitor introduced me to Bloom's taxonomy (Bloom et al., 1956). Here the broad categories, which set up a hierarchy from knowledge at the base, through understanding and application, to evaluation and synthesis at the peak, were appealing because they were illustrated by test questions. Here was an analytic tool that could be used, reactively to study what one had been doing, proactively to plan to do better.

These encounters left me puzzled. If we were to take aims seriously, how radically would we need to change if we were to accomplish what, in our justifying our rhetoric, we claimed to be doing? There was also the problem of specificity—how precise and detailed did you have to be in this process of following through on your intentions? I was to find ways of answering these questions through an unexpected and serious involvement in school physics.

Putting Aims First

Early one afternoon in spring 1967, I was ushered into the office of the director of the Nuffield Foundation, which supports research and development work in science, medicine, education, and public policy. The room was impressively splendid, being part of a small mansion in Regents Park in London, which was at that time the foundation's headquarters. I was a little overawed by the ambience, but far more overawed by the business that had led to my being invited to come up from Birmingham for a discussion—or, I asked myself, was it more like an interview for a job?

A Nuffield project to fashion a new curriculum for advanced-level school physics had been in existence for about a year, and had collapsed as the loss of confidence in the work of the team whom the foundation had appointed had led to the resignation of its organiser, followed by resignation of the entire team. This was a crisis for physics education. The academic advisors, whose loss of confidence had precipitated the collapse, could not themselves design a curriculum for the schools, and the foundation was dependent on the goodwill of teachers because adoption of their curriculum innovations was entirely voluntary. Projects in biology, in combined physical sciences, and in a separate course in chemistry were well under way. The physics gap had to be plugged, and urgently.

The solution that was being explored was to appoint two joint organisers. One was to be a teacher or teacher trainer identified with the school sector, outside but close enough to the original team to understand the merits and failings of their work. I was invited to be the other: I had good credentials as a university physicist, whilst it was also judged that from my informal work with schoolteachers and a formal role with an examination board, I would have some understanding of and sympathy with school curriculum innovation.

This was a risky enterprise for me. It would interrupt my university career, to my detriment unless I achieved significant success. The prospects of such success did not seem rosy, given the fractured context from which the resurrected project would start, and the threat of tension between giving sympathetic support to the impetus to reform amongst schoolteachers, and the need to reestablish the credibility of any reform with my university peers. A great deal would depend on the relationship I could develop with the other joint organiser—if we were to disagree and start a power struggle, all would be lost, yet I hardly knew him. On the other hand, there was a moral imperative—I cared about physics education and could see, pride and megalomania apart, that I was well placed to help save the day.

This project was in the second generation of curriculum reform ventures supported by the Nuffield Foundation. The initiative for the first generation, which had worked on the secondary curricula for ages 11 to 16, had come from the science teachers themselves. They were dissatisfied with curricula that had hardly changed in content for half a century and were lacking in interest for students. The foundation was influenced by evidence that the recruitment of students to advanced courses in science and engineering was declining at an alarming rate.

A key figure in the pre-16 physics reform supported by Nuffield was Eric Rogers, an Englishman whose approach to teaching at Princeton, set out in a remarkable but bulky text with the characteristic title *Physics for the Inquiring Mind*, had attracted much attention. His overarching ambition, to help the school pupil to be a "physicist for the day," appealed to my own wish to see physics teaching aim at some form of "authenticity." Rogers gave strong emphasis to learning for understanding, and to integration of practical work that put pupils in touch with phenomena and then raised questions about how models might explain these. Overall, he had clearly defined aims and showed others what it meant to take them seriously (Jennison & Ogborn, 1994).

A long talk with Jon Ogborn, the proposed fellow organiser, reassured me that our personal styles and our visions for the reformed curriculum were sufficiently in harmony. His good relationships with the original team held out promise that some of their members, who were amongst the best possible physics teachers for the task, would join us, thus helping us to reassure the community of physics schoolteachers that they had not lost their stake in the enterprise.

The list of aims, which was the first goal of the new team's work, contained six components, as follows:

1. Learning in the future
2. Understanding physics
3. Understanding the nature of physics
4. Learning to enquire
5. Awareness of the role of physics in the world
6. Enjoyment of physics

These were clearly broad and ambitious, and the struggle was both to turn them into practical reality in the classroom and to reflect and reinforce them through the examination. Thus, for example, for aim 5 one approach was to use real-world problems as the starting point for a topic, to create a context of significant problems: thus a piece on the inevitable exhaustion of the world's supplies of fossil fuels if the developing world were ever to reach the per capita energy consumption of the United States led into a study of energetics and the Second Law of Thermodynamics. For aim 4, many practical exercises were designed to serve in the exploration of theoretical ideas, and an individual experimental project was to form part of the assessed work of each student.

What followed from our commitment to taking these aims seriously was that they demanded a systemic approach, one in which aims, curriculum design, pedagogy, assessment, laboratory equipment, and the teacher's capacities were all intertwined in a complex and recursive interaction and not in any simple linear sequence. The various issues involved in such a list will be taken up in later chapters. The meaning and the very existence of each aim were continually being questioned as we tried to realise them in concrete practice—and it was rather surprising that our original list of six survived largely intact (Black & Ogborn, 1974).

Pursuit of these aims also required attention to the future needs of the students taking advanced-level physics. In thinking about the fifth aim in particular, we had to see this in the context of data on their postschool careers. We had to recognize that only 15% went on to take specialist physics degrees. Most went on to study other sciences, or engineering, or medicine. And what aims could be justified for the 20 to 25% who usually failed the final examination?

The experience of all of this work was refreshing. From my involvement, I became more confident and more radical about the task of improving teaching. One had first to decide on the general aims that should drive the strategy. Then one had to work systemically at the interlaced complex of constraints and opportunities, with flexible readiness to learn from experience underpinned by resolute commitment to the driving aims.

Into the Big Time: Aims for Everyone?

The involvement in the Nuffield project strengthened a transition in my interests, from physics research into science education. This led to a final discontinuous step when I moved in 1976 to become the second head of a Centre for Science Education that my predecessor had founded within Chelsea College, one of the colleges of the University of London. One of my new tasks was to be educational consultant to the body responsible for the whole spectrum of the Nuffield school science courses, which assumed the name of the Nuffield-Chelsea Curriculum Trust.

The Nuffield curriculum enterprise had burgeoned. The first courses were for the academic "grammar-school" pupils at the pre-16 and then at the specialist post-16 level in the separate sciences. In a later development, courses for the "less able" and a primary science course were constructed. The need to think about curricula that might be suitable for all students across the 5 to 16 age range forced me to look more deeply into my assumptions about aims. It was clear that courses based on the main concepts of physics were unsuitable for many, being conceptually demanding, lacking the grounding in action and experience from which abstract understanding might develop, and lacking interest because of their irrelevance to pupils' daily lives.

I became more sharply aware of the dilemma entailed through my reading of David Layton's (1973) study in which he described the struggle in the late 19th century between those in the United Kingdom who wanted the newfound school science studies to be devoted to a science of common things, and the high academy, who wanted "real science." The academy won, and Layton pointed out that in most of the Nuffield innovations that victory was still leaving its mark. My main reaction to this—in part defensive—was that education in science had to convey what science was and what scientists did. To fail to do this was to mislead pupils and to fail to transmit this important part of our culture. Of course, as I increasingly realized, it was difficult—so we just had to try harder.

Then, again quite unexpectedly, both the aims agenda and my contact with David Layton came dramatically to the fore. It all started in spring 1978. A group of about nine of the Chelsea Centre staff sat in my room engaged in hurried and difficult debate. A few days beforehand we had heard indirectly that tenders were being sought from the government Department of Education and Science (DES) for conducting large-scale national monitoring surveys of school science performance as part of the work of their new Assessment of Performance Unit (APU). For some reason our Centre had been left off the original circulation list. So we had only obtained the documentation with nine days to go to the deadline, having heard that rival institutions had already been preparing their bids for some time. We had to make a bid, but we were under stress not only because of the shortage of preparation time but also because we had difficulty with the DES document, for we judged it to be ambiguous, inconsistent, and in one important respect misconceived. Our dilemma was whether to go along with the specification and suppress our misgivings, or whether to prejudice an already hurried bid by a critique of the specifications for the monitoring.

Our bid was short-listed, so only two weeks later, on a cold, clear morning, I and three of my Chelsea colleagues were walking across the Thames on the Hungerford Rail Bridge, with the trains lumbering past us causing our pedestrian walkway to vibrate beneath us. We were not confident. We had taken the high-risk route of criticising the ministry brief, having concluded that its serious conceptual confusions would come to haunt anyone trying to work to its framework, and we wondered whether this would rule us out. However, this also made us more bold, for since there was no point in trying to please by dancing to the tune of the ministry, we were going for broke as the guys who had new and better thoughts to offer.

To my surprise, we succeeded. We were offered a joint contract with a group at the University of Leeds led by David Layton. The ensuing project entailed frenzied activity. There were the deadlines to have tests in schools for set dates every year from 1980 to 1984; tough conceptual struggles, among ourselves and then with the ministry's monitoring committee; the practical struggles to formulate quality test questions; and the need to write for and talk in the public arena to achieve the trust of a teaching profession that felt suspicious and threatened by this government initiative.

Our main problem with the original brief was the issue of content versus process. Initiatives in the United States, as worked out, for example, in the SAPA (Science as a Process Approach) curriculum, had influenced British thinking, notably in primary science courses. These concerns had to be resolved within the first task for the project, which was to think through a framework of aims to provide the criteria for the assessments. We ended up with a list of six categories:

1. Recording and Representing Data (graphs, tables, charts, etc.)
2. Measurement—use of instruments
3. Observation
4. Applying Concepts—within the three subareas of biology, chemistry, and physics
5. Planning Investigations
6. Carrying Out Investigations

Whilst these were aims for an assessment survey, they had to reflect the curriculum so that the outcomes could give a meaningful portrait of the achievements of school science education in order to be interpreted as the "official aims" for school science. This status, flattering but yet worrying to those who feared the coming of national control, was further enhanced when we came to results, illustrated by exemplary questions and samples of pupils' responses. These influenced teachers by putting flesh on the bones of the abstract aims, thereby making them more meaningful and, to many, both appealing and feasible. Thus, as several commentators later pointed out, the science APU turned out to be a curriculum development exercise disguised as an assessment project (Black, 1990).

The rationale behind this list was that only category 4, Applying Concepts, would involve specific content but that the others would assess processes only and might not depend on the content that pupils might have studied. In this respect, the process movement, despite its problematic validity, served a purpose because the government was not in a position at that time (1978) to determine syllabus content, and given the wide diversity of the courses followed in schools, we could not assume common content in national survey assessments. So we had to engage in difficult debates to specify a least common denominator of content for each of the three assessment ages (11, 13, and 15).

Whilst the process bias was partly adopted for political convenience, it had some important consequences. One was that there was considerable emphasis on practical work. We argued that the aims could only be assessed with apparatus prepared and used with several thousand pupils, a prospect that doubled the budget originally set out in our contract bids. The justification was that if we could not report on these aims, this would have the effect of making practical work seem of small importance in school science. The ministry swallowed hard and agreed. In consequence, the importance of hands-on practical work was reflected in our work, and this helped in the promotion of support for this aspect of science education. In this respect, we were far ahead of the corresponding American surveys conducted by the National Assessment of Educational Progress, which was not then funded to conduct practical testing. I was able to see at first hand, on a visit to the United States, the scope and limitations both of the NAEP work and of similar programmes in some of the states.

Ironically, our innovations in supporting the process emphasis through formulation of assessment examples also taught us that the content–process division was misconceived. As we interpreted pupils' responses in all of the categories, seen clearly through our use of open-ended items, we discovered that the reasoning they used always involved their ideas about the content and context of the question—the content-free test was a myth. Thus, for example, most pupils would perceive a question presenting for comment data about (say) fish as requiring some knowledge of fish, not as a test of (say) pattern recognition in data for which one's knowledge of fish was meant to be irrelevant.

An outstanding example was in Observations, category 3, where some first argued that any pupil observation, be it scientifically relevant or trivial, ought to earn assessment marks, a dilemma we could escape only by arguing that we were looking for "scientific observation." However, we then had to say that observation was only a scientifically useful process when the inevitably selective acts of observation were informed by a scientific model, which would guide the selection. A final report on the project concluded that category 3 should have been a subset of category 4 on Applying Concepts. Such conclusions had particular relevance for the development of primary school science, for it helped to undermine the support for "process-only" science and helped influence the later work of several of us at primary level (see chapters 2 and 6).

Aims, Professional and Political

Many suspected that the APU exercise was a first step toward government control of the curriculum. There was rising dissatisfaction in government with the state of school education. It was felt that there was a lack of clarity of purpose in much of primary school work, whilst at secondary school level schools had been struggling with the consequences of the abandon-ment in the 1970s of a selective and stratified school system. The newly established comprehensive schools faced new problems in providing cur-ricula suitable for the whole ability range. These problems were intensified by the raising of the age limit for compulsory education to 16 in 1973, for many pupils near the leaving age were impatient to get into the "real world" of employment rather than to work at their learning. Optional courses proliferated, and as schools tried to invent courses relevant to daily life and employment for pupils who were not succeeding in the diluted aca-demic curricula, they were criticized for providing their pupils with an inadequate education.

When in 1987 the government determination to establish a national curriculum was set out in legislation, leading science educators were called together to advise the minister on a suitable curriculum specification. I was not involved, being concerned simultaneously with a group working on national assessment. Those involved in the curriculum work brought to the table beliefs about combined science in place of separate subjects, about the process–concept union, about a vision of authentic investigations in prac-tical work, and about the importance of teaching about the links between science, technology, and society. Their recommendations set out a vision of a course in science, to replace the separate sciences, and to be taken as a double subject by all up to age 16, an issue to be discussed in chapter 3. They included open-ended investigations as a requirement, but also broad-ened the aims of the science curriculum by including separate targets on the history and philosophy of science, on the applications of science, on science technology and society, and on communication in science. There had already grown up small-scale curriculum projects aimed at adding to the existing curricula some new studies of science and society, some with focus on historical issues, other on current developments in industry, technology, and the environment. It was on the basis of these that the science educators were impelled and equipped to formulate specifications for learning in these areas for inclusion in the national curriculum.

In the public consultation that followed, these innovative ambitions aroused controversy, and the final outcome lost or attenuated some of these features, but was still radical. As the implementation got under way, wor-ries about overload amongst teachers were matched by a sense of excite-ment that new aims were on the agenda. However, for a variety of reasons, mainly to do with muddle over assessment rules, the curriculum was soon revised. Here a minor tragedy was played out, mainly within the discus-sions of a small group selected by the ministry and briefed to reduce the load of material in the curriculum. Predictably but sadly, the old priorities reappeared. The reduction was achieved by removing almost all of the innovations, the only survivors being the double-subject combined science for all and the pupil investigations. The investigation component itself narrowly survived a later attack by the independent schools whose prestige with right-wing politicians gave them influence out of proportion to their numbers. The lesson was that to introduce radical change too quickly was to risk not only a return to the status quo, but also the provision of spurious evidence for critics who could say, "We tried that and it didn't work."

Seen now in retrospect, this was a muddled and sadly flawed development. It reinforces the view expressed earlier that whilst aims must be put first and taken seriously, the matrix of issues within which they might be implemented is all important. When national policy is being reformulated, the pressures of competing interest groups, and of political expediency that pushes for hasty advance with inadequate backup, followed by equally hasty retreat under fire, become all important. Then the prospects of an educationally sensible solution may be fairly slim unless the ground soil of public and political opinion has been very carefully tilled.

Still Debating

Now, in the new millennium, the debate about the best form of a science curriculum still continues. My involvement in the OECD project opened up wider lessons about the curriculum, notably that concerns were shared across many countries and that it was no longer taken for granted that scientists had the first and last word in deciding about the orientation of school science. These experiences are described fully in Mike's account.

My personal involvement as one of the many advisors to the formulation of the American standards for science education was a replay of many of the British experiences—but with important differences (National Research Council, 1996). The total time devoted to the formulation, consultations, and reformulations was over three times longer, and a far wider group, including many more teachers, were drawn in. Another notable feature was the emphasis on inquiry as a central feature for pedagogy in science, to be reflected in resources, training of teachers, and assessment. This was similar to the British emphasis on pupils' investigations, but broader in implications for a whole spectrum of teaching and learning activity.

One problem remained. None of these had gone as far as enthroning a science for everyday life, Layton's "science of common things." It was still not clear what "citizens' science," as opposed to "scientists' science," ought to be like, let alone whether it should have overruling priority. A group sponsored by Nuffield explored this very issue in the United Kingdom, attempting, with a report published in 1999, to open up debate in advance of a promised revision of the British national curriculum for the year 2000 (Millar & Osborne, 1998). That report set out cogent arguments for taking seriously the broadening required if the aim of "science for all citizens" was to be a real rather than a cosmetic commitment. It pointed out that to take it seriously we would have to contemplate a quite new structure and quite new forms of pedagogy for school science education. However, the political imperative was to make minimal changes to the status quo, and to be conservative rather than radical in curriculum matters. So Britain started the new millennium with the old aims still firmly in the ascendancy.

JOINT REFLECTIONS ABOUT AIMS AND POLITICS

If the continually changing aims of science education during the last 100 years are an indicator, it must seem to the attentive bystander that new sets of goals are always just around the corner. Teach science to make people better thinkers. Teach it to help children love nature. Teach it so that they know how scientists do research. Teach it so that people understand how science plays a role in their lives. A given set of priorities in science education lasts for about 20 years, give or take a decade. (Object Teaching lasted a bit longer, the post-Sputnik reforms a bit less.) But the chances are pretty high that there will be new priorities 10 or 20 years from now.

The inevitability of change poses special challenges for everyone involved in providing science education: teachers, curriculum developers, test makers, evaluators, teacher educators, and many others. Change is always arduous. Changing all the elements of a system at the same time is especially difficult. Continual change can be almost incapacitating, in that it breeds feelings of discouragement and futility, even cynicism.

So what to do? What stance does a teacher take to keep the system functioning positively for students and the society? Or a school administrator? Or an educational researcher? Or a teacher educator? Most of the options don't seem attractive. Stay current: Change curriculum and teaching styles to reflect the latest aims. Resist the changes: They are untried on a large scale and may cause more harm than good. Ignore the changes: Enthusiasm will wane, and practice will revert to something like the present. Employ the new rhetoric with parents and colleagues: Change little, though, since a wide range of practices in the classroom can be matched to any set of goals. In fact, few of these choices are professionally satisfying or morally justifiable—and in reality, actual options are not so stark. Some of those involved in and with the educational system and who are committed to serving students might feel that they have little choice but to stay abreast, consider the possibilities, and make adaptations—as good sense, personal predilection, and opportunity permit. Others might feel different-ly, impelled to take action to make or shape changes rather than merely to cope with them.

One way to view the stories and perspectives proffered in this chapter, then, is as historical context for considering new aims as they compete for public and professional attention and acceptance. But, in addition to serv-ing as sources for reflection about contemporary developments, they also can inform action. This chapter, after all, is largely about commitment, our own and others.' Those who feel moved to make a difference will be act-ing out personal aims, the only question being whether they do so con-sciously or unconsciously, overtly or covertly. The enthusiast who acts out of individual commitment can be invaluable in any enterprise, but can also be dangerous if the basis of that commitment has not been thought through in the light of past experience and the needs and interests of those who are to be affected by it. History provides no road map. It does help, however, in calibrating one's professional compass. With luck, it also helps to damp-en the fluctuations.

One characteristic of both our careers is that, mostly by accident, we have been engaged in such a variety of communities and contexts that we have been both inspired, and given opportunities, to innovate, and at the same time warned about obstacles and complexities. Thus we have been caught up in action, both proactive and reactive. In a small way we have been able to exercise a principled opportunism, just as, on a larger canvas, figures such as Zacharias in the United States and Rogers in the United Kingdom had a profound influence through grasping opportunities offered by shifts in the public and political moods of their times.

Our Conclusions

We may or may not have done wisely, but we have learned some lessons about such work. One is that one person can contribute significantly to the tide of events. It has always, for us, been worthwhile to respond to the moral imperative to do something, while at the same time looking around very carefully lest one be the proverbial bull in the china shop. Another les-son is to be prepared—to be patient, to encounter unexpected obstacles and opponents, and, if not to fail, at least to achieve no more than a mod-est success. Pursuit of any nontrivial aim is more like a marathon than a sprint, and pursuit of it when the enterprise is in the political and public arena is more like a mission to convince people to give up smoking than an effort to get them to buy a new detergent.

If there is one outstanding theme that will recur throughout this book, it will be the study of change in education. The formulation of clear goals is but a first step in a commitment to change. Such goals have to be fleshed out in a feasible curriculum, fashioned in relation to the wider aims of school or college education, brought to life in both classroom instruction and assessment, supported by research, and above all taken to heart by teachers so that they become part of their commitment to their students. We shall explore all of these elements in the chapters that follow.

2

Curriculum Development

Curriculum changes to fit the times. So do styles of curriculum development. Before World War II, and for more than a decade afterward, the actual development of course materials was almost exclusively in the hands of textbook publishers. Typically it was the publisher that identified the need for a curriculum change and the emphasis it should take. The publisher then recruited authors, usually, in the United Kingdom, from experienced schoolteachers, but in the United States more often from the ranks of college professors of science education, augmented usually by classroom teachers and, sometimes, the science community. For these people, textbook writing was a part-time (and highly profitable) commitment.

In the late 1950s, the pattern shifted quickly and fundamentally. In the United States, with the entrance of the National Science Foundation into the science education field, the curriculum *project* became the locus for development. The impetus for the establishment of the NSF in 1950 came from scientists heavily involved in wartime work where the proven method for accomplishing large tasks (like the development of radar and the atom bomb) was to create working groups of experts who devoted their energies full-time to the job. Consciously or not, the wartime experience provided the model. Top-level scientists were to be central in creating the new curriculum programs, which often were characterized by revolutionary expectations (and uncommon levels of self-confidence). At many levels, the effects on science education were profound.

The NSF had both the money and the prestige to create such projects, which it did with vigor for more than a 10-year period beginning in the mid-1950s: the Physical Sciences Study Committee (PSSC), the Biological Sciences Curriculum Study (BSCS), the Earth Sciences Curriculum Project (ESCP), and many more that by 1960 would include projects at the elementary school level as well. These were hugely expensive efforts by curriculum development standards. They were funded by the national government. They had unprecedented influence. And they changed the way people thought about curriculum for decades.

In Britain, the genesis and evolution were different. The professional association of science teachers started projects on their own, because of their dissatisfaction with existing frameworks and materials. Finding that the work could not be done with only the spare-time efforts of their members, they tried to obtain funding to free up the time of teachers who might lead the projects. The government felt at that time that public funds should not support curriculum development, but with the encouragement of several leading scientists, it helped to convince a private trust, the Nuffield Foundation, that curriculum development in the sciences merited support with substantial financing. This was a triumph for the teachers, but a mixed one because the foundation decided to manage the development projects itself, so that the teachers' organizations lost control. Nevertheless, the teams that did the work were mainly drawn from practicing teachers, although in the steering groups that provided oversight of the development teams, some leading academic scientists played a powerful role. These scientists gave generously of their time and support. On one occasion, it was their dissatisfaction with the work of a project team that led to resignation of the team and a fresh start to the work.

In this chapter, we describe the workings of these projects, highlighting their achievements and styles of operation and the issues they raise. The latter include, for some of the more prominent examples, the "ownership" of science education (including levels of teacher participation); evaluation of science curriculum; links among curriculum, pedagogy, and assessment (envisaged or not) in the planning; and the implementation of educational innovations. Furthermore, the fact that curriculum development work of comparable scale and ambition is no longer prominent raises a larger question of whether the underlying vision was seriously flawed, or was simply of its time and no longer appropriate.

MIKE'S STORIES

New Content for Elementary School Science

The first two grants by the National Science Foundation for curriculum development work below the high school level were awarded in 1960. One went to Robert Karplus, a physicist at the University of California, Berkeley, for a project called the Science Curriculum Improvement Study (SCIS). It emphasized concepts for second graders (7-year-olds) such as frames of reference (ways in which the motion of a passenger in the seat of a speeding car seems different to an observer inside the car than to one out-side) and how interactions at a distance (as between magnets) work and might be explained. The other grant went to the University of Illinois for a project on astronomy directed by Wyatt and me.

Astronomy content below the high school level was largely descriptive at the time. The students were informed that Earth is at the center of the solar system, nine planets orbit the sun, Earth has one natural satellite, Mars two, and Jupiter twelve (four of which go in a direction opposite to the others). The solar system is disc-shaped. Seasonal change is an effect of Earth's tilt on its axis. Eclipses seen from Earth are the result of shadows cast by Earth (in the case of a lunar eclipse) or the moon (in the case of a solar eclipse). The sun is very far away, about 93 million miles. It is one of many millions of stars in a collection called a galaxy. Our home galaxy is named the Milky Way. It, too, is disc-shaped. There are many millions of galaxies. There wasn't much more.

Wyatt and I pointed out that this array of factual material provides lit-tle indication of which ideas have more intellectual mileage than others or how people obtain such information. Furthermore, it gives no intimation of the types of problems to which today's astronomers devote their careers. We proposed to develop a course for students ages 11 to 14 that would help them to understand some of the major concepts that astronomers themselves consider fundamental to their field. The NSF had never before awarded a grant for a project directed by a professor of education, but the fact that Wyatt and I were to be co-directors was sufficient to meet what was then a tacit but firm operating principle, which conformed with the prevailing view about who should determine curriculum content for ele-mentary and secondary schools.

The aims of the new course and an outline of the core content were hammered out in detail during the first summer of the project, in 1960. In the spirit of the times, and with enthusiasm on everyone's part, the scien-tists in the group—and the scientists alone—deliberated about what belonged in such a course. The core group was joined for extended periods during that first summer by Robert Karplus and Owen Chamberlain, both physicists from the University of California, Berkeley, the latter a Nobel Prize winner. It was a sign of the times that such scholars were moving into the curriculum field by the dozens.

One of my deepest impressions of the summer's deliberations was how enormously challenging it was at a conceptual level for the astronomers and physicists to outline a course for young students. Daily meetings went on for eight weeks while first one approach, then another was considered. This inability of outstanding scientists to forge a quick and straightforward consensus about the astronomy to be taught to people 11 years old was one of the most lasting lessons of the astronomy project for me. It helped to make me permanently skeptical about many of the curriculum passions I heard about from scientists in the succeeding decades as they proffered their solutions for the continuing problem of "reforming" science education. With significant exceptions, most of their remedies consisted of nostalgic reification of the science education they themselves had received during their school days. I knew that problems of selecting curriculum content were not resolved that simply.

About halfway through the summer discussions, agreement began to form around the idea that it is very important for students not only to understand whatever important astronomical concepts we will have identified, but also to begin to comprehend how those concepts came to be accepted by the scientific community. For that to happen, they would need to know in appropriate detail about the evidence brought to bear to defend one point of view or another—about different models of the solar system, for example, and how that evidence was factored into whatever consensus developed.

I am sure we were influenced in that decision by an event that had occurred during the preceding summer just up the road in Woods Hole. (The astronomy project met each summer on Cape Cod in Massachusetts because it was easier to persuade outstanding people to come there than to east-central Illinois in July.) Many of the people involved in the new curriculum movement in science and mathematics had met under the auspices of the National Academy of Sciences. The purpose was to become acquainted with one another and begin working through some issues common to their various approaches. This meeting of about three dozen figures closely associated with the new curriculum movement proved pivotal. A psychologist, Jerome Bruner, was a key organizing figure and the one designated to write a short monograph about the conference. *The Process of Education,* his distillation of the major ideas (Bruner, 1996), is still in print. That report encapsulates much of the thinking about curriculum construction for the science and mathematics education of the time and was instrumental in disseminating the movement's underlying philosophy.

Among many other points, the participants in the Woods Hole Conference declared that each discipline has an internal "structure" that could be comprehended even by young children. Bruner's report contained several soon-to-become aphorisms, such as, "We begin with the hypothesis that any subject can be taught effectively in some intellectually honest form to any child at any stage of development" (p. 32). And, "The decision as to what should be taught in American history to elementary school children or what should be taught in arithmetic is a decision that can best be reached with the aid of those with a high degree of vision and competence in these fields. To decide that the elementary ideas of algebra depend upon the fundamentals of the commutative, distributive, and associative laws, one must be a mathematician in a position to appreciate and understand the fundamentals of mathematics" (p. 19). Further, "It may well be that the style of thought of a particular discipline is necessary as a background for learning the working meaning of general concepts" (p. 28).

We in the Illinois project were imbued with such ideas. The first two were implicit in the way we conceived and organized the project. The last became increasingly explicit as we developed the curriculum. By the end of the first summer, the astronomers developed a story line in which the main thread stressed the manner by which humans have come to accept what we now know about the structure and workings of the universe. It was almost a guiding rule: Little content was to enter the course for which the students could not also understand how the knowledge was derived. For example, in the first of the six short volumes of about 90 pages each that we developed, *Charting the Universe* (Atkin & Wyatt, 1969), we essentially told the story of how it was possible from Earth to make a scale model of the solar system without knowing any of the absolute distances, and how humans learned to estimate distances to the stars. To do so, we taught a great deal about angles, parallax, and apparent size. Since we could not assume that students in upper elementary and lower secondary school grades had been taught the necessary geometry (the subject is usually introduced in high school), we included many pages on triangulation and on similar triangles. It was the first time that I had to deal seriously with issues about relationships between science and mathematics.

The second volume, *The Universe in Motion,* provided the basis for understanding the fact that the sun is at the center of our system of planets, not Earth. This was done not by assertion, but by helping students grapple with the evidentiary basis for an Earth-centered system and the conceptual conditions that had to be satisfied for the heliocentric model to replace it. The students must understand, we believed, why Tycho Brahe, a contemporary of Copernicus's with the most and best data, rejected the Copernican view until his dying day. In the third booklet, *Gravitation,* a theory was presented that was able to account for much astronomical motion. Again we had to introduce a considerable amount of mathematics so that children in the upper elementary school grades would have a grasp of the concept of constant acceleration.

In developing a story line for astronomy with considerable reliance on the historical development of certain ideas, we paralleled some of the thinking in Harvard Project Physics. This project, led by James Rutherford, a former high school teacher, and Gerald Holton, a historian of science at Harvard, was developed at about the same time as PSSC, but did not garner quite so much attention in the field. In both our project and the one at Harvard, though, we clearly thought there were clues to helping students understand some key ideas in science if they better grasped how the ideas were developed over the ages. To teach Newton's laws, for example, it might be helpful for students to understand why they were not intuitively obvious to the many brilliant people who thought about such matters before Newton did. They simply could not break away conceptually from the fact that friction is ubiquitous. It was an important lesson about scientific breakthroughs.

Who Owns Science Education?

In the course of little more than 10 years, I had moved away from my deep commitment to Mrs. Billhardt's integrated curriculum, in which students studied about the social and political consequences of inadequate sewage disposal and what to do about them. I was now part of the new and prestigious Brunerian world, in which the responsibility of defining the essence of the science curriculum passed to distinguished members of the academic scientific community. Beyond my opportunism, the intellectual excitement of the new curriculum movement was palpable, and the fact that the NSF was providing the dollars for curriculum development enhanced the attractiveness of such activity for some of the nation's scientists.

But *should* the decisions about what to teach at the elementary and secondary school levels be left primarily to the scientists? If so, should it be those at the leading edge of university-level research, or should it be those who focus on teaching at the college level? What about scientists from industry and government laboratories, who may more likely focus on content that relates to human needs and wants? Or should it be some combination of all three? And what about the teachers of the students who will be served by the curriculum? They work in the classroom every day and presumably know more about the vagaries and demands of curriculum and pedagogy. Should it be experts in science education, those who study the subject, write about it, and conduct research, typically professors in schools and colleges of education?

These questions are both consequential and contentious. Depending on the answers, the curriculum can look quite different, as was noted in the first chapter. A research-oriented scientist may identify the core concepts that underlie his or her discipline as central to the course, as in PSSC, UICSM, or the astronomy project. Fundamental ideas that possess powerful generality, like atomic structure or the molecular foundations of biological processes, for example, might be featured. The scientist from industry might stress the applications of some overarching scientific principles to human needs and wants: how concepts in chemistry are put to work to create new products, for example, or how they can be used to increase agricultural productivity. A teacher may have a bias toward those topics that show greatest promise of engaging the largest number of students. Since school science is widely disliked by the majority of students, a teacher may want to stress the role of science in daily life to enhance motivation. A professor of science education may try to emphasize topics on which education research has focused, for example, the development of the concepts of inertia and mass.

The content favored by these groups is not necessarily incompatible, but the resulting curriculum can and does look quite different depending on who makes the decisions about content selection. What are the governing principles for choosing one over another? What are the guidelines? Where are the priorities? In what form do the controversies about such matters arise? At the time, I gave little thought to such fundamental questions.

"Implementing" a Curriculum

I wasn't the only one. Notably muted in the style of curriculum development that began to take shape in the 1950s and 1960s were influential roles for teachers in the content selection phase of the creation of new courses. They did have one key function, however. The new materials for students, typically new textbooks, had to be tested in classrooms to be sure they worked. The typical procedure for field-testing, as in the Illinois astronomy project, was for scientists to prepare the new materials during the summer in experimental editions. These drafts and the accompanying laboratory material would then be sent out to selected school districts where teachers and school administrators had agreed to participate in classroom tests.

Often the districts were chosen because of their representative quality (urban and rural, rich and poor, ethnically homogeneous and racially mixed) and their willingness to cooperate in evaluating the material. Each project developed its own procedures for obtaining teacher and student reactions, but the NSF invariably expected and supported this type of field testing. It would add both to the usability and credibility of the new program. Questionnaires were employed extensively. Most projects also dispatched teams of teachers to provide assistance in the classroom and observe the experimental curriculum in action. Based on reactions from the field, the writers would reconvene during the following summer, often with some of the teachers present, to revise the materials in light of the year's experience. Most projects went through several such cycles—four in the case of the astronomy project—before versions were ready for general publication and distribution.

The end result frequently was not pleasing, however. Many scientists involved in curriculum development were appalled when they saw the materials they had prepared actually used in the classroom. Too often, the teacher knew the words but mangled the tune. Investigations by students of wave motion in a ripple tank sometimes were transformed in the classroom into a lecture by the teacher (occasionally without the ripple tank!). Or sometimes students read directly from the new textbook, taking turns reading the paragraphs. The students in such classes had little opportunity to develop the depth of understanding that the scientists believed comes only with deep and direct contact with the phenomena. The carefully wrought courses often seemed to propagate a level of science understanding that was little better than the programs they were trying so hard to replace. In language most of them came to regret, some scientists proclaimed that henceforth they had to concentrate on "teacher-proofing" the curriculum: Be sure that the project's final materials could not possibly be used other than as the creators intended, even by the least imaginative of teachers. Films and film loops were produced by the projects not only to aid the teacher but to try to direct their pedagogy. Detailed texts and guides for teachers were written. Both the "teacher-proof" characterization and the concept of teacher-as-faithful-implementer later came to epitomize what many people saw as the arrogance of this style of curriculum development. Furthermore, it did not work very well. There did not seem to be much of a market for courses that represented major shifts in educational philosophy and science content.

Not that other methods of translating dramatically different and new curriculum ideas to the classroom worked much better. In the astronomy project and some others, teachers were regular members of the summer writing group, but usually for the express purpose of developing the teacher guides that would accompany the new curriculum, and little more. Thus the teachers employed by the project were seen as links between the scientists and the thousands of other teachers who would be using the new program but who had no direct association with the developers. They had little or nothing to do with selecting the core concepts in the course.

When I accepted directorship for a major publisher's textbook series in science at the conclusion of the astronomy project in 1966, I tried to incorporate some of the concepts and approaches used in the NSF-supported activities. I invited a physicist, an earth scientist, and a biologist to join the group. I also persuaded the publisher to bring in professional science writers. Because the publisher had an established distribution network, the curriculum may have reached more classrooms than many of the

NSF projects (and certainly more than the astronomy project). It also was more modest in what it attempted conceptually than the NSF projects. Still, it fell far short of blazing a path with respect to teachers using the books as the authors hoped. Nor, in the end, was it a commercial success.

Curriculum Development in the OECD Countries

It wasn't until the 1980s that the educational policy community arrived at the general view that "linear" models of curriculum development just did not work. One could not prepare a curriculum outside the classroom or school and expect the teacher to adopt it faithfully for her own class. Sometimes the adaptations by the teacher enriched the program by bringing in local issues and examples, but often there was only a superficial resemblance between the intentions of the curriculum developers and the curriculum that took shape in the classroom. By the late 1980s, those in curriculum development projects and those who developed strategies for educational change generally were trying to devise new curriculum models and new models of educational change.

The OECD project was conducted in the early 1990s, and offers illustrations of how strategies for educational change were themselves changing. Each of the 13 participating countries chose one or more innovations in science, mathematics, or technology it considered particularly important. Among the features studied in each case were the strategies employed for changing science, mathematics, and technology education. We found that there was a clear trend. In all the countries, even the one with the most centralized educational system, Japan, greater responsibility had devolved to the teachers themselves for making the changes, not solely in devising methods of teaching, but also having a greater role in the selection of content. In fact, only one of the 23 initiatives selected for close examination in the 13 countries employed the basic 1960s plan of assigning scientists the sole responsibility for content selection.

Teachers Working Together

The innovation chosen by the Germans was one in which an integrated science approach was taken for students in grades 5 through 10. Teachers in one of the states, Schleswig-Holstein, had originated the program. They sought and received assistance from professors at the University of Kiel, but the basic curriculum structure was one they devised because they believed it most suitable for the students they taught. Momentum developed for adoption of the curriculum largely through teacher-to-teacher contacts. The university served as a hub for discussions about the new curriculum, with professors remaining in largely a consultative role. Ultimately the new curriculum received the imprimatur of the education unit in the federal republic, and the innovation spread to almost all the other states.

In Spain, teachers were faced with a new law that extended the age of compulsory education. They knew that they soon would be teaching students who, if precedent were a guide, would have chosen not to continue their formal education in science. The decision was made to move to integrated science. The responsibility for the new curriculum fell largely to the teachers, this time through explicit policy on the part of the Ministry of Education. General guidelines were prepared in Madrid, but they provided for most of the development work to take place within the dispersed regions. Teachers met regularly, school by school, to decide on what would be taught and how.

Japan has a stronger history of central control than Spain. In 1989, the Ministry of Education developed a new elementary school curriculum in "Environmental and Life Sciences." The curriculum was developed in close consultation with selected teachers and scientists. It was somewhat more detailed than Spain's, but teachers in each prefecture met to decide just what shape the curriculum would take in their own region. In the case of Yokohama City, a large committee was created with three representatives from each school. The committee refined the guidelines from Tokyo, and specific plans were drawn up. These, in turn, were brought to the individual schools, where they were tried and modified.

The California story was similar to Spain's. The state adopted a new framework for science in 1990. Integrated science was suggested. With federal funding and additional support from the National Science Teachers Association, which was also promoting integrated science, ten "hubs" were established around the state. High school teachers from the ten regions met regularly to hammer out just what content should be selected, and how it might be taught. In one of the cases on mathematics education innovations, the teachers in just one school developed a new curriculum for their students that then spread nationally via commercial publication.

North Carolina runs a public, residential high school for students with high capability in science and mathematics. The students are chosen from all over the state to specialize further in these subjects during their junior and senior years. The teachers in the mathematics department decided they needed a new pre-calculus course. They determined further that it should be based entirely on applications. All content was screened rigorously on the basis of that criterion. The result was excision of several topics traditional in such courses—conic sections, for example. In this case, there was a backlash from some university-based mathematicians who believed that content central to their disciplines was being underemphasized. They were all the more concerned because the intended student audience as a group was especially able in mathematics and science.

By the end of the century, then, there had been a pronounced change in the role of teachers in curriculum development from the practices employed universally during the Sputnik-associated reforms. In the post-World War II programs, university-level research scientists were the sole determiners of the content to be taught. Teachers participated in figuring out how it might be presented to students, usually by trying experimental versions in their classrooms and providing feedback. By 2000, several of the new and broadly used programs had little or no direct participation by scientists.

Why the Shift Toward Teachers as Determiners of Content, and Is It Desirable?

There are several possible reasons for the new role for teachers. For one, schools rapidly were becoming more inclusive at the secondary school level. In Spain, Britain, and many other countries, the age of compulsory education was raised. In the United States, a higher percentage of the age cohort was attending secondary school for four years than ever before. In 1939, about 25% of people then 30 years old had done so. By 1985, the percentage had jumped to 75%. While the 25% dropout rate is of serious public concern, it nevertheless represents a phenomenal increase in school attendance. Furthermore, students of the 1990s are far more polyglot; in some school districts, the students speak more than 100 different languages at home. The educational consequence is that schools must serve a much broader base of the population, and for a longer time. That responsibility falls to the teachers. Successful adults tend to remember their own education favorably. However, basing school reform on such nostalgia may not be effective policy in an age when the school population is larger as a percentage of the population, and much more diverse.

Another reason for the reduced influence of scientists may be that fewer of them decide to participate in education improvement below the university level at the turn of the millennium than before. The requirements for advancement in an academic career in science have escalated. Securing funds for research is a central and time-consuming task. Competition for academic posts is much sharper than it was in the 1950s and 1960s, when universities were expanding rapidly. Professors are less willing or able to pursue other professionally related interests.

On the other hand, the National Academy of Sciences has turned impressive effort to issues associated with school improvement. It may be that that agency will succeed in reviving scientists' commitment to school improvement. Certainly that is the intent of those within the organization who are working hard on such issues. It remains to be seen, however, if even the cachet of the most prestigious of American science institutions can mitigate the kinds of pressures that most academic scientists feel so keenly.

Yet another factor may be that scientists have been trying to improve science education for more than 40 years. The public is told, and many people believe, that the results have not been commensurate with the investment. Scientists of the 1960s may have thought they could make marked improvements rapidly. They have learned that there is no quick fix, any more than there is for other social problems. So the job is being left to those who make their careers in teaching.

Such an outcome would be unfortunate. The improvement of science education is a national priority almost everywhere. It takes a range of talent, commitment, and other resources just to keep from moving backward. While that may be a discouraging message for those who could make important contributions and want to see the results of their efforts quickly, it may be time to acknowledge it. It appears that the public has come to understand that in some fields, like protection of the environment, it takes steady work to stay in place.

PAUL'S STORIES

Taking It for Granted: Physics Is Physics, Isn't It?

My "taken for granted" view of the content of teaching was brought home to me when, after six years of research in a multidisciplinary crystallography unit at Cambridge, I was asked to teach an advanced course in solid state physics in the physics department at Birmingham. What I chose to include was left to me. I knew what the conventionally regarded textbooks contained. However, I also realised that the texts were about a quite small group of solids: most of the crystals that my colleagues in my former crystallography research unit—notably mineralogists, protein chemists, and metallurgists—had been studying were not even mentioned. So a collection of chapters about ionic crystals, a few of the metallic elements, even fewer of the intermetallic compounds, and a few semiconductors—that is, about those solids for which physics research had made some progress—was self-evidently a treatment of the physics of solids.

What was striking was that this limitation in scope was not discussed in these texts, so that a student would not be made aware of how the subject had been framed. Furthermore, it was not clear that such an agenda best served the needs of the whole group of undergraduates. Thus this first experience of constructing a course made me realise that a curriculum did not appear as ready-made or predetermined. It was a product of somebody's decision, grounded in this case in the concerns of a particular research community.

Designing Teaching In-House: Content with Method

As I advanced in seniority, enhanced responsibility opened up opportunities to work with colleagues to develop a more comprehensive view of the undergraduate curriculum as a whole. There was amongst the faculty a very creative and radical group of about my own seniority who shared a concern that to achieve our overriding aim, to produce effective professional physicists, we should concern ourselves less with content and more with some radical changes in the methods of teaching and learning. Thus in one change, a particular topic was removed from lectures and taught only by laboratory exercises with individualised programmed learning. In another, "pick-and mix" collections of laboratory experiments were replaced by structured laboratory-based courses, whilst open-ended experimental projects came to play a key part in all three years of the course (Black, Dyson, & O'Connor, 1968; Ogborn, 1977).

The senior professors who had managerial responsibility were worried because these innovations were making demands on the staff, so that they had less time for research. Yet they could hardly suppress the enthusiasm of staff when the innovations could be seen to be authentically valuable physics. I can see in retrospect that our group was unusually fortunate in the extent of their forbearance. In most of this work we were fairly free to develop our innovations. This was quite different from the world of school physics, where I was learning that public examinations constrained, indeed determined, the curriculum.

Going in Deep: The Shock of Complete Immersion

In the work on Nuffield A-level physics, the formulation of the aims described in chapter 1 was but a start. I came to this task knowing all too little, either about serious curriculum development or about the reality of school teaching. One early lesson, that serious curriculum development had to be systemic, optimising within a complex of constraints, has already been discussed in chapter 1. The problem was to navigate this complex without losing sight of the main aims. The core of the solution had to lie both in the teaching methods that we could promote, to be discussed in chapter 4, "Pedagogy and Learning," and in the selection and articulation of the content. These latter aspects is central to this present chapter.

A very important feature of the project was considering new candidates for inclusion in the content to be studied. Two novelties were chosen to pay attention to the need to emphasise the world of applied physics and the interests of those with their sights set on engineering. One was a systems approach to electronics. Out went thermionic valves and any attempt to keep up with the continuous development of silicon-based devices; all was to be focused on finding out the input/output properties of devices and circuits, regarded as "black boxes," and then using this information in the design of assemblies of these elements to compose devices to perform certain useful functions. Another novelty was to introduce induction motors, partly on the grounds that there were far more of these in everyday devices than of the conceptually simpler types taught in the old curricula.

However, more subtle problems arose as we tried to introduce some of the key ideas of 20th-century physics that had revolutionised the subject but had hitherto been regarded as too "advanced" for the school curriculum. Here we were influenced by the work in the United States of two high school projects, the Physical Sciences Study Curriculum (PSSC) and the Harvard project. We shared with PSSC the influence of Bruner, in his dictum that one should be able to teach any concept to pupils at any level.

One of these key ideas, wave-particle duality leading to the wave-mechanical theory of atoms, was thought essential because it is the basis of our understanding of matter. The other, the Second Law of Thermodynamics, seemed necessary because it underlay much of chemistry and engineering as well as of physics, and because it was the key to understanding the world energy crisis so that it could serve to connect with serious issues of social and environmental concern. At the outset it was not at all clear how, or even whether, such topics could usefully be taught at all at this level without their being bowdlerised. We achieved notable success, mainly through the creative genius of my co-director, Jon Ogborn.

In waves and particles, our approach was to engage students whose mathematics could not come near to coping with the analytic solutions of the Schrödinger equation in finding a solution by a numerical incremental method that could be used to explore graphically the possible wave shapes to represent an electron in a hydrogen atom. The same technique was introduced earlier in the course as a simple way of looking at graphs for such concrete laboratory examples as the classical simple harmonic motion of the pendulum. Thus we could show the continuity of the new theory with conventional methods of analysis, whilst also bringing out the implications of the radical idea of a wave model for electrons. This was a breakthrough in what French authors were beginning to call "didactic transformation."

For the Second Law of Thermodynamics, a statistical approach led to the big ideas through the playing of games with dice, showing that when random processes operate within certain constraints there emerge powerful general rules that govern what can or cannot happen. Through such arguments, pupils could come to understand that it is inevitable that energy will be dissipated, and thus that when energy-rich fuels are burnt the energy will be spread around so thinly that it will not be useful anymore (Black & Ogborn, 1978).

There was considerable pride in these achievements, and the teachers collaborating in our trials shared our excitement. However, we had to spend considerable time with university physicists, both to check that we had not committed some deep errors in our simplifications, and to secure their support as we presented our novelties to sceptical audiences.

These particular innovations were the exciting high peaks. Less dramatic was the work of making the parts fit into an overall connected structure. Here there were two considerations. It was important to implement a variety of entry points into the different topics. One way was to revisit familiar laboratory exercises in the context of tackling new problems. Another was to start from everyday problems to explore what physics might contribute to an understanding of them. The guiding principle was to ensure that each entry point would arouse curiosity whilst also giving an authentic lead into the main physics ideas to be explored. Overall, the team also wanted an intriguing variety, for one of the aims of the course was enjoyment of physics. At the same time, it was also necessary to so plan the sequence of topics that it would be possible to bring out, in later work, uses, and therefore consolidations, of earlier work.

In some cases, new approaches could be even thinkable only if a piece of equipment that was affordable and yet workable at school level could be invented, so the team would struggle with ways to measure the velocity of light, or the numerical value of the constant in Coulomb's law for electrostatic attraction. Where such struggles succeeded, we then had to produce a prototype and convince some commercial manufacturers to produce a few copies quickly for our trial schools, thus investing in unprofitably small numbers in the hope of large orders to come if the course were to achieve success. The time delays involved here meant that decisions about these novelties had to be taken at a very early stage, so preempting later argument.

There were indeed many complications in respect of timetables. For a course to be trialed, schools had to be selected and times set out well before the materials were ready. Then the various strands had to be brought together so that the trials teachers could be briefed, would have the necessary equipment, the necessary written materials, and adequate time before they had to start teaching. In addition, of course, we had to ensure that an appropriate examination was in place well before the end of the trials peri-od (a task to be described in chapter 5). These problems of the logistics and rough practicalities of curriculum development received no attention in the educational literature on curriculum development, which seemed to us to be written by those who were far removed from the actual job. As we nav-igated this maze of systemic reform, we came to regard curriculum devel-opment as a form of engineering, for it involved the meeting of a need in an optimum way with the best resources that could be obtained within the time deadlines, and with a product that would be workable within the con-straints of the contexts for which it had been designed.

This was clearly top-down curriculum development. Our approach avoided some of the worst pitfalls of top-down development by having experienced teachers make up the majority of the team, and by the process of trials, initially in about 30 schools, in which the needs of the trials teach-ers were taken seriously, and their findings fed back into revisions before anything was published. Nevertheless, the team formed an in-group who were designing clever new things for others, and then had a substantial problem to convince those others that the ideas could be used in their prac-tice and that it was worth the bother of helping the team to work out how to do this. On the other side were some distinct advantages. A full-time team had the time and opportunities to brainstorm crazy ideas as a group, and could also visit a range of experts to help check out, and even gener-ate, radically new approaches.

The complex web of requirements could only be put in place because we had the prestige of the Nuffield Foundation behind us and could prom-ise that our course ideas would be taken up by a sufficiently large propor-tion of schools that commercial investments in new publications and equip-ment would prove rewarding. In its maximum growth from 1977 onwards for several years, the course and examination were taken by almost 10,000 students each year—which was then about 25% of the total entry in the country for A-level physics—whilst there was also significant influence as syllabuses and textbooks for other courses were revised. It is unlikely that any local developments, initiated and owned by the teachers for their own courses, could have made such an impact.

Overall, this experience of curriculum development was exciting, enjoyable, and deeply rewarding. Of the many lessons about curriculum development that it taught me, the most significant were:

- it can be a very demanding intellectual exercise, stretching to the full one's grasp of the subject matter;
- to achieve serious aims requires both a radical appetite for a voyage of adventure and a tight control on the steering;

- it is an exercise with many dimensions, and with fiercely constraining logistics, so that an engineering systems approach is needed for effective planning and execution;
- of the many constraints, that of matching the possibilities to the needs, and the freedom to change, of teachers is the one that calls for the most careful and constant attention.

Another reward was that adoption of the course in a large number of schools continued for 30 years, until its recent replacement by a worthy and radical successor.

Building Curriculum on Firm Foundations: Nuffield Primary Science

As explained in chapter 1, my work with the APU led me to engage with the process–content debate that had been influential in the primary science curriculum. Both my deputy director, Wynne Harlen, and myself came to believe that the assumption that one should teach science as process skills only, with no attempt to teach any concepts, was impossible in principle. When she left King's College, University of London, to take a chair at the University of Liverpool, we started to formulate together a proposal to research this idea in a project that came to be known as the Science Processes and Concepts Exploration (SPACE).

The approach was founded in the constructivist paradigm, which had emerged as a new influence in science education research. Its message was that one had to start any teaching by exploring the learner's own prior understandings and then fashion work to help the learner transform them. To overlay them by merely imposing new truths would not work. The project therefore had two main priorities. The first was to research the prior understandings of children in the age range 5 to 11, given that existing research had attended mainly to older children. The second was to analyse key science concepts in order to tease out those ideas that were simple enough yet could provide a basis for later learning of the productive conceptual structures of science. Thus, for example, in looking into the nature of light, the ideas pursued were the representation of phenomena by straight lines on paper (rays), the distinction between primary and secondary sources, the formation of shadows, and the notion that in order for one to see rays of light from that which was to be seen had to enter the eye. These were difficult enough and, ironically, many such ideas had been either taken for granted or dealt with as fairly obvious in most school textbooks for high school science (Black et al., 1992).

We obtained a grant from the Nuffield Foundation and secured, through their Local Education Authorities, the collaboration of schools near London and Liverpool. The work was carried out by the volunteer-teachers who first talked through our ideas with us. On the basis of evidence that they could evoke about pupils' ideas, intervention tasks were proposed: These were experiments, questions, and problems that were designed to challenge children's ideas, and through which they could be guided to suggest new ideas and/or to test any explanations they might offer for observations that were inconsistent with their initial ideas. The task of the research staff was to design the starting tasks and the intervention activities, together with appropriate assessment tools, to train the teachers, to observe and support the implementation in classrooms, and to collect the data so that learning gains could be recorded and interpreted.

Over three years of work, we were able to develop some tried and tested methods that showed that the approach could succeed. In addition, results enabled us to decide which of our proposed "elementary concepts" could be grasped by children and which could not. These data, supplemented by details about how the results changed with the age of the children, enabled us to formulate an achievable curriculum of science concepts for the primary age ranges.

We now had something that had not been achieved before—a researched basis for a curriculum development. It had been our stated intention throughout to use the research in a subsequent curriculum project, and in the last year of the project there was much negotiation with potential publishers. The outcome was joint funding between the publishers and the Nuffield Foundation for a project to produce teaching materials to support a new primary science course.

One problem was that our approach was based on ideas and support for the teachers in developing active participation by pupils. Books for pupils had, at best, a secondary role; indeed, we were concerned lest any pupils' books would become textbooks and lead to science work on paper only, lacking in pupils' involvement in practical activities and in discussion of ideas. We did produce a rather unusual set of books for pupils. Each provided short reading pieces on different aspects of the science topics, mainly adding interesting stories or ideas to complement the main learning work and to link with other primary school subjects. However, the main burden of the teaching approach had to fall directly on the shoulders of the teachers.

The Nuffield group had developed strategies for dissemination and aftercare of its projects. In the case of primary science, local user groups for the materials were set up; meetings were organised to brief teacher training institutions; and one of the development team was given part-time support to coordinate such work, in close collaboration with the publishers whose sales representatives could be an important source of feedback from the schools. The collaboration with teachers in the development not only ensured practicability, it also meant that there was available a group of teachers fully conversant with the use of the course in practice who could help in its dissemination to others.

Takeup was slow, in part because teachers found the description of the approach to the understanding of science concepts rather complex and, lacking confidence in their own grasp of science, preferred schemes with simpler recipes based on pupils' books where the matters to be learned were set out for them. To improve matters, the general texts giving guidance for teachers about the approach were rewritten, and an entirely new booklet was produced for teachers, explaining in simple language with much visual material the science ideas explored in the course.

These continuing evaluations, and adaptations in response, helped ensure a steady growth, so that unlike most new project materials, these have risen steadily from a low base rather than enjoying an initial surge by novelty and then fading away. This growth has been helped by recognition that the course is unique in having been built on the basis of a research project. Overall, at the time of writing, the story of Nuffield Primary Science is still unfolding. It is typical of practical curriculum development that, as for my earlier account of Nuffield A-level physics, it is hard to tell the story without knitting in the issues of pedagogy and learning, of teacher development, and, in this case, of research.

A New Model for a Very New Aim: Nuffield Design and Technology

The curriculum for Design and Technology had long been an area of confusing variety and contention, so that when it had to be defined as one of the required subjects in the United Kingdom national curriculum in 1988 there ensued a lively debate. The consensus that emerged established a subject with a firm basis in the notions of practical capability, and in active involvement of pupils in designing, making, and evaluating. The interest here is that this development throws new light on the nature of the science curriculum. Some of the other fundamental issues will be taken up in chapter 3.

Very few teachers had been trained for or had gained experience in this new approach to the subject, and the provisions for retraining were inadequate. The first report of the national inspectorate about the early implementation of this curriculum was highly critical. The problem that we puzzled over with the Nuffield Foundation was whether we could do anything about this situation. We were clear that we should try, for several of us argued that if this new subject could survive its serious teething troubles, it might well become a radically helpful innovation. The vision was that it might shift the balance of the curriculum toward practical and applicable activity to offset the undue emphasis on the academic and the critical in most other curriculum areas. The problem was whether, through the provision of printed curriculum materials, we could do anything to help a subject that should be focused on practical activity and not on the reading of books.

Our debates led to a proposal to produce, as core materials, ring-binder files containing detailed specifications of suitable tasks. A typical task might require a pupil to design and make a "cool" hat for a teenager, or a buffet meal for a small party, or a workstation for a pupil's bedroom. We already knew that teachers had considerable difficulty in thinking up tasks suitable for a design-and-make curriculum, and tended to grasp at the straws of anything seen to be achievable rather than to make a cool headed choice between the multiple virtues and drawbacks of several alternatives. A good task would have to call for and help develop practical skills, and to require tools and materials of as high a quality and level of sophistication as schools could reasonably manage. It had nevertheless to be so open to a variety of solutions that there was room for students to develop creativity and design skills, and it ought to draw on ideas developed in other school subjects, notably mathematics, science, art, and possibly also geography, English, and history.

The core file, Open Tasks, was to be supported by general guides for pupils and for teachers, and by a Resources Guide. The idea behind this last item was that students and teachers would need a single reference source about the many items, both in content knowledge and in skills, that might be needed in a technology project. Examples were properties—of metals, wood, plastics, fabrics, and foodstuffs; techniques of cutting, shaping, joining, and treating different materials; techniques for electronic or pneumatic control systems; methods for construction of load-bearing structures and of mechanisms; and advice about various approaches to design, to modeling, and to product evaluation.

The plan was sufficiently convincing that both the Foundation and a publisher were prepared to share the risk of contributing the substantial funding involved. Having cleared this main hurdle, our other hurdle was to find a director who might carry through this daunting yet exciting venture. We were very fortunate to appoint David Barlex as full-time director and the work commenced under the supervision of a three-man junta, David, Geoffrey Harrison—a professor of technology education with whom I had worked on earlier projects—and myself. We met regularly, most of the work being done by David as the full-time director. As time went on, first my contribution and then Geoffrey's became less important as the framework became firm and David took full control. Under his skilled and creative direction, consultations, writing, and school trials led to an unusual and compelling set of publications (Barlex et al., 1995).

The structure of these publications was a novel one, designed to implement solutions to three main problems. First, for the provision of well-documented ideas for open-ended design-and-make tasks, the problem was that, given wide freedom of choice, pupils would not even think of using techniques of which they were ignorant. However, to provide a set of training exercises where techniques were to be taught out of context would be in conflict with the main ethos of the course. The solution was to provide two types of tasks. The new type was called Resource Tasks: In each of these, a realistic problem was presented but the constraints were such that certain techniques had to be used, and so would be learnt in the context of a particular product serving well-defined purposes. The original Open Tasks remained as before, although each could now be indexed in relation to relevant Resource Tasks, which could be undertaken beforehand or in an intermission during the open task. This device was attractive—and indeed it became a requirement when our idea for these two types of task activity was subsequently adopted as part of a revision of the National Curriculum.

A second problem was to produce the Resources Guide, a thesaurus to which pupils could turn for help with strategies, tactics, and techniques. This had to be accessible and intelligible to pupils from age 11 upward. It would have been easy to cover everything needed in a 1,000-page textbook, but this would have been too expensive and probably too difficult to use. The eventual product was a 250-page text. Brevity and intelligibility could only be attained by very smart use of diagrams and tables, with a minimum of text in simple language, and with the double-page spread as the unit within which a self-contained piece of work could be set out and viewed without breaks in turning pages.

The third problem was to ensure that pupils had a clear overview of the unusual structure of the course we envisaged, with its interwoven elements of Open Tasks, Resource Tasks, and the Resource Guide, the whole to be seen within the overall aim of developing practical capability and understanding of the nature of design and technology. Since the approach would also be new to most teachers, it was thought essential to address pupils directly. So a pupils' book was produced. Half of this book was text to explain the rationale of the course, the nature of design and technology, the approach that a student should take to the work, and the criteria for quality in design-and-make exercises so that pupils could begin to monitor their own progress. The other half served a different purpose. It consisted of short accounts of technological developments, some contemporary, like the development of the domestic washing machine; some historical; some high-tech; and some about alternative technologies used with success in developing countries. These were presented for study to complement the hands-on activities. Such study was seen to be essential, in part to emphasise that consideration both of ethics and of fitness for purpose, in the social context for which a technological solution had been designed, is a prime criterion in the task of meeting human needs.

The publication of the course materials was accompanied by the setting up of local groups of teachers, with schools involved in trials of the materials forming the core, and with a full-time field officer appointed to support dissemination. To date, the course materials have been bought by more than half the secondary schools in England and Wales, and they are commonly referred to as setting the standard for the implementation of Design and Technology in secondary schools. Trials are also under way at the time of writing of materials for primary school work in this subject.

The above story raises issues that might come in time to be central to the science curriculum. If the curriculum for school science education is to be designed with serious intent to meet the needs of all in their adult life, then it must cover a range of perspectives relevant to the place of science in their lives and in their cultural inheritance. This range should include some understanding of the methods and the excitement of science, a grasp of at least some of the most enduring and fundamental concepts, and an understanding that science is a product of the struggles throughout history of individuals and society to understand and perhaps control their natural environment, contingent on that history yet objective (in the need for confirmation by empirical evidence as a key to success). There should also be some acquaintance with the ethical and resource problems raised by the practice of science in our society today.

It is hard to believe that such a rounded study could be brought off in a curriculum that still tried to get through the set pieces of current content-bound syllabuses. The Nuffield study for Science 2000 came to a conclusion like this (Millar & Osborne, 1998). Its proposal, that the science curriculum might well be built around a series of what it called "stories," bears strong resemblance to the way in which Design and Technology is built around open tasks. In both cases, the elements have to be articulated so that through working at them in sequence, the resource components required will build up a useful basis in knowledge and understanding of some basic concepts and methods—albeit fewer than are tackled at present.

It is significant here that the experience of working well outside the science curriculum context had led me to think in a fresh way about the familiar science territory. The task-resource model was a new way of thinking about the curriculum, which both opened up new prospects and exposed some of the covert assumptions of my earlier work. What had become commonplace to me was to think of the curriculum as having a core of concepts to be covered, and outer layers of application work and other possible areas for learning tasks that might enrich or open up the core learning. The basic change was to regard the involvement in a holistic task as an important learning experience in its own right, so that the core material and the task elements should be partners with equal status. The corollary was that parts of the core could be disposable—one could always learn later, indeed one will always have to be learning later.

JOINT REFLECTIONS ABOUT CURRICULUM DEVELOPMENT

Several factors influenced the approaches to curriculum development during the period from 1940 to the start of the new century. A brief list would include the Depression, World War II, the fact that higher percentages of the student cohort were attending school after the war (and for more years), the political decision to launch major efforts to improve education for the poorest children, and the expansion of educational opportunities for people beyond 16 or 18 years old. All of them, and many others, had their impact on what was to be taught and how curriculum was created. Textbook companies, national curriculum projects, and governmental initiatives all operated in somewhat different ways as each moved in (and out) of a dominant position on the curriculum development scene. As we review what we have written, however, it becomes clear that one feature in particular seems to have stood out for us as we look back: the influential role played by outstanding, academic science researchers in addressing the key issue of identifying the subject matter that should be taught to students in elementary and secondary schools.

This realization gave us pause. We began to wonder if this possibly unique circumstance in the history of science education was indeed the most crucial one in trying to put the period in perspective. A sizeable number of scientists of extraordinary stature within the scientific community certainly devoted themselves virtually full-time in the 1950s and 1960s to curriculum development. Like almost everyone else, the two of us were impressed. Their involvement added luster to our own choices to enter the field of science education. Furthermore, we both were just getting started in our careers at the time, so the impact on us was particularly powerful. Indeed, it may be the case that Paul would have continued to pursue his interests in crystallography if a sizeable number of respected scientists were not also reorienting their careers toward deeper involvement in education. Rereading our stories, in fact, the influence on us of the activities of the prestigious scientific community in the field of education was so great that we seem to have used this phenomenon as a touchstone against which to gauge almost everything that came before in curriculum development and everything that came after. What happened as the influence of scientists in curriculum development waxed and waned? What was the result? And later, how did the role of teachers expand in choosing science content for the curriculum? What forces were at work? How was the curriculum different?

Our Conclusions

In puzzling over what we have chosen to write about and trying to figure out why these events stood out so powerfully for us, we came to the view that the circumstances of the 1950s and 1960s may not represent the most fruitful frame of reference for thinking about either the present or the future. If the period was rare, even singular, it would be an error to speculate about trying to resurrect what we saw then and try to integrate it with other forces and developments that we see now. To attempt to craft guidelines for policy and practice based on the presumption that a comparable infusion of talent and vigor from the science community in the early 21st century would occur and again make a significant difference might not be the crux of the matter.

Such a development surely would be salutary. Significant participation by scientists in matters of improving science education is not only useful but also necessary. In fact, it isn't difficult to note significant forces exerting influence toward such an end as we write. The National Science Foundation and the Nuffield Foundation, for example, continue to play active roles in providing funds for education improvement. Enhanced education of undergraduates in the sciences and mathematics is a priority at many universities in both countries; university presidents, chancellors, and deans are speaking out more about the quality of college-level science education in the new century. University departments seem to be highlighting their teaching obligations for all their students more than they have in the past. Such activity well might spill over to elementary and secondary schools. But is that the most useful kind of lesson to be drawn from our experiences and the main trend to be amplified and expanded?

If it were, these concluding paragraphs would examine, for example, the implications of the events we saw in the OECD project on innovations in science, mathematics, and technology education wherein teachers began to have strong and direct influence on the curriculum as they tried to tailor their teaching to a more inclusive student body. How might the two crucial sets of actors—academic scientists and classroom teachers—collaborate most effectively? We would examine, for another example, what happened when teachers became more assertive about their prerogatives in selecting science content for the curriculum, when the science taught began to highlight the relationship between science and its manifestations in the lives of all citizens, rather than the science that was deemed fundamental by the leading science researchers. What were the shortcomings, as well as the advantages? We would try to build on what both of us have learned from the encouraging recent initiatives of the National Academy of Sciences that heighten involvement by leaders of the science community in improving science education in the early 21st century.

However salient such analysis and speculation might be, we have concluded instead that the matter of ownership of the science curriculum and how it is and might be distributed, though far from trivial, is not the central issue. Just as the creators of some of the post–World War II science curriculum projects were dismayed when they saw how their programs in physics, earth sciences, biology, and mathematics actually were used in many classrooms, others sometimes have been appalled by the quality of some integrated science curricula and other programs designed to relate the science curriculum to societal issues. In the former case, it was disappointing to see the science taught as new facts to be memorized (and then forgotten), often with little understanding of the elegant, conceptual scientific structures that the scientist curriculum developers were trying to emphasize. In the latter case, integrated science designed to address "real-world" phenomena often wasn't integrated at all. It consisted of parallel studies within the conventional disciplinary boundaries with little attempt to highlight connections. Curriculum programs that related science to societal problems often dealt more with the societal programs than with the relevant science—and frequently oversimplified the science to make a point about how it might be applied (points that the reader will encounter more fully in the next chapter). In fact, for us the preoccupation with *who* designs the curriculum that we displayed in reporting on our experiences with curriculum development may have been a red herring across the path of trying to understand even more consequential factors in improving the quality of science education than parsing the influence of two important groups—university-based scientists and classroom teachers—and trying to merge their contributions.

If we are correct that ownership of the science curriculum, however fascinating and important in our own careers, is not the central question, that any program can fall seriously short of its creators' best intentions when it plays out in actual classrooms, then where do we look for clues toward improvement? The trail toward raising the quality of science education, for us, seems to lead not to any single set of factors, but instead to the full range of influences on the quality of science education: carefully considered and reachable goals, adequate instructional materials, suitable equipment, support for teachers, and much more.

Within this array, however, we have come to believe that it is the teachers themselves and their vision, thoughtfulness, beliefs, and abilities that overshadow virtually everything else. It is what they do with students in the classroom that is at the heart of the condition of science education during any period. Do they help students understand the major ideas as well as the evidence that supports them? Do they help students understand the gap between their present understanding and the norms of accomplishment toward which they are trying to strive? Do they create settings wherein students begin to fathom their own capabilities to understand and engage in scientific activity? Do they provide timely assistance as students begin to grapple with complex ideas? In short, do they teach complex, scientific phenomena in an intellectually honest manner? These general criteria for gauging the quality of science education programs strike us as of enduring importance. Just as some teachers can defeat the aims of any science curriculum, others can create constructive and productive educational settings and experiences for students from a wide variety of curricula and instructional materials, even those that may seem impoverished. It is not that curricula and instructional materials are not important. They are. But the quality of teachers and teaching is the heart of the matter. Improving that quality is the goal toward which all initiatives to strengthen programs of science education should aim. It is a point to which we will return.

3

Subject Matter Boundaries

The common pattern at the secondary school level in the United States and the United Kingdom is to teach separate courses in biology, chemistry, physics, and earth sciences, usually with little attempt to underscore connections among these disciplines. Rarer yet are attempts to teach about links between science and other school subjects such as history, economics, or art. In the United Kingdom, the list of prescribed subjects is set out in legislation as if they were both freestanding and self-evident. When Paul was deputy chair of the National Curriculum Council, he tried to foster a general curriculum discussion. The chairman suppressed the suggestion and advised privately on a later occasion that he had been instructed to do so by advisors from the Ministry. To engage in such talk would, in their view, be academic indulgence, get nowhere, and slow down the process of putting the new curriculum in place. The formulation of national standards in the United States is also approached subject by subject, with no overall plan. Yet there are other ways. For example, the curriculum documents produced in both Norway and Finland set out a clear, inclusive educational and curriculum philosophy, so that it is possible to discern, for science as for other subjects, their specific contribution to a general conception of the purpose of schooling.

But if there were such a comprehensive curriculum plan, how should the boundaries of the science curriculum be drawn within it? In practice, science has not always had a place in the curriculum solely to teach science as the term is usually understood from within the discipline. There is sometimes a focus on the applications of science in daily life. Sometimes the boundary expands to include social issues, like controversies about the uses of nuclear energy or environmental degradation. Such programs are often described as science/technology/society (STS) courses. Then, for one more example, there is integrated science, by which is meant that the disciplines are not taught separately but together, perhaps by centering on cross-disciplinary themes like transfer of energy (which can be studied in physical and biological systems), patterns of change (which can range from cosmology to evolution to human development), and systems (which might include feedback concepts in electronics but also self-regulating biological systems, both internal and external to an organism). What assumptions underlie such varied approaches? What merit do they have? How have they worked?

For students, science lessons are embedded in a daily schedule that includes lessons on other subjects. The way they are presented often results in students erecting mental boundaries among these different subject fields. Is this the best we can do? Are the subject disciplines solely a collection, a tower of Babel?

Such questions raise a variety of problems, from the deeply epistemological to the pragmatics of school schedules. In this chapter we attempt to frame the debate by examining some aspects of the curriculum in which our experiences have led us to think across the boundaries of the science curriculum. The intention is to establish the case for further deliberation, and to indicate some directions in which it might be pursued.

MIKE'S STORIES

Informal, Yet Rigorous: Learning from England

I was 40 years old in 1967 and had never been abroad when Max Beberman of "new math" and UICSM fame suggested that he, I, and another colleague at the University of Illinois who specialized in elementary education pay a visit to schools in England. Beberman was becoming interested in younger children. He had started to raise questions about the math-for-math's-sake movement he had started, wondering how it comported with what theorists and many teachers were saying about education for children younger than high school age. It was a time of modest resurgence of educational progressivism: There was talk about the "whole child," which meant, to oversimplify, that educational programs respond to and capitalize upon the developmental needs of children, that subject matter be fitted into the natural patterns of childhood and not the other way round, and that the best way to prepare children for the adult world is to make education significant for them at whatever age they happen to be.

Americans were beginning to read about educational changes in

England that reflected child-centered approaches. *Crisis in the Classroom* (Silverman, 1970), a widely noted book, criticized the sterile and mechanical learning he and his wife saw in many American schools. A prominent feature of *Crisis* was a laudatory view of some English primary schools. The "infant schools," in particular, were portrayed as places where children were freed to engage actively in a level of learning that seemed to make the 3 R's–based education in the United States lifeless by comparison, at least for young children. (English primary education was separated at the time into "infant" schools for children ages 5 to 7 and "junior" schools for those from 7 to 11.) The term "integrated day" was used in England at the time to suggest that time slots were blurred and that children and teachers moved smoothly across the subject fields in studying events and objects that were part of their lives.

Many American educators were inspired by what they read and heard. Schools were established in Philadelphia, New York, and elsewhere expressly modeled on what their originators had seen in England. The ideologies and philosophies that drove such developments were not foreign, however. John Dewey had written in the 1920s and 1930s about a curriculum for all schools centered on real-world issues in which students would learn how knowledge drawn from the separate subject matter fields could be employed in addressing issues in the community. Knowledge of the disciplines was a priority for Dewey, but he believed it should be introduced as children coped with problems that arose in daily life. Mrs. Billardt surely was influenced by such ideas. So was I.

By the late 1960s, though, there was a pronounced shift toward placing a reconceptualized view of the structure of the subject disciplines at the center of the curriculum, in the style of Bruner's Woods Hole manifesto. In this perspective, but earlier, too, progressive ideas and practices were coming under fire as not sufficiently attentive to the subject disciplines and naïvely centered on romantic views of childhood associated, in their origins at least, with Jean-Jacques Rousseau: Children's natural development, if appropriately nurtured, would lead them to constructive learning activities. Actually, caricatures of this educational philosophy had appeared as early as the 1930s. A cartoon, not atypical, portrayed a teacher of primary school children as asking her class, "Now what should we do today, children?" Dewey was much upset by such characterizations, though there were no doubt some teachers who fit the picture. For him, subject matter integrity was of paramount concern, and he wrote at some length about the matter in the mid-1930s in response to such interpretations of his educational ideas (Dewey, 1938). Many admirers seized the English infant school development as an opportunity to highlight what Bruner's subject-based approach seemed to be missing.

Square Children

Beberman had heard that some of the child-centered, primary schools in England that Americans were reading about also taught significant mathematics, and that is the feature that intrigued him. There might be polarized positions being debated in stark terms—"teach the subject or teach the child"—but when Beberman heard that the two views could be reconciled, he wanted to know more. Apparently the English schools were moving far beyond the usual diet of computational arithmetic. They were teaching real mathematics—and within a child-centered framework.

Our actual school visits over a three-week period were organized by Edith Biggs, one of Her Majesty's Inspectors and a specialist in mathematics education. At the time, there were about 400 inspectors for elementary and secondary schools in England and Wales. A major role they had assumed was to identify, support, and amplify good educational practices all over the country. They did so largely through school observations and consultations, supplemented by special programs for teachers. Almost always, inspectors in primary and secondary schools had been successful classroom teachers themselves. That fact, plus their regal titles and terms of appointment, accorded them considerable standing, credibility, and professional independence. (This state of affairs was not to last long. In the mid-1970s, the national government started to move the Inspectorate away from the advisory and consultative service it had become toward reconstitution as an agency for school accountability. By the mid-1990s, it had virtually ceased to exist.)

Steered by Biggs, we went to about half a dozen primary schools in London, Bristol, Nottingham, Swanage, and rural Oxfordshire. We were impressed. Children age six and seven were detecting mathematics in just about everything. At the Sea Mills Infant School near Bristol, for example, when we entered the building the children were in a large room measuring their respective heights and arm spans. Some of the children were lying on the floor with their arms outstretched. The children told us they found it easier to measure accurately when those to be measured were lying down. This was not solely an exercise in measurement, however, for the object of the activity was to learn if there was a consistent relationship between the distance between the opposing fingertips of outstretched arms and a child's height from head to toe. Charts were being prepared for the different children as they measured one another. This led to some full-scale drawing of prostrate children, and then to large graph paper were the children learned to represent their data in a form that helped to reveal underlying relationships. Height was graphed on one axis and distance between outstretched fingertips on the other. It turns out that most of the children were pretty nearly square—their arm span was about the same as their height—a fact that delighted the children as well as the observers.

Graphing was not a topic usually taught in American elementary schools until students were about 11 or 12, and then ordinarily not in mathematics but to represent some set of interesting relationships in science or social studies. At Sea Mills, there were no sharp divisions among the subjects. Mathematics (and something about human growth patterns, working in small groups, and investigating an unknown phenomenon) was learned along the way to finding out about some other inherently interesting relationships.

Government Encouragement

We saw many more examples of the integrated day on that visit. In Eynsham, Oxfordshire, the entire school seemed to be involved in a cleanup of some kind. The mathematics included charts that were being made to record the amount of trash being collected over a period of a few weeks as people in and around the school were increasingly sensitized to the cleanliness of their surroundings by the children. Again they were graphing, this time to show that less trash was collected as more people became aware of the project. At Eynsham, also, we saw our first school without formal classrooms or internal walls. All the five-through-seven-year-olds were in one large room with the head teacher and about 10 additional teachers. There were alcoves framed by low bookcases and a large space in the middle, but it was easy to see just about everyone in the room. The children seemed to know where they were to be at any particular time. In the English infant schools we saw, apparently space was integrated along with the subject matter.

The movement was gaining some momentum in Britain, including government encouragement. *Children and Their Primary Schools* (Department of Education and Science, 1967) was published in two volumes as a government document detailing the practices, research, and theory that buttressed a child-centered view of primary education. Popularly called the Plowden Report after its chair, the first volume provided many examples and much of the justification for such an approach to the education of young children. Almost the entire second volume was devoted to documentation about what was happening, including assessment and evaluation results. Children in integrated-day programs (in about a third of English infant schools at the time, we were told) compared favorably in conventional subject matter achievement with students in traditional schools. It was an uncommon and impressive level of documentation for a report on an educational innovation.

The Movement in America

The American Ford Foundation became interested in these developments. Harold Howe, a former U.S. Commissioner of Education and dean of Harvard University's School of Education, headed education at the foundation at the time. Ford provided funds for me to return to England in 1969 for two months. I continued to be impressed with the quality and depth of the subject matter learning I saw, which seemed reminiscent of Mrs. Billhardt's classes 15 years earlier. Soon afterward, I served as one of several advisors to a Ford-supported project that produced about two dozen short monographs, later assembled in three volumes and published both in the United States and the United Kingdom (Anglo-American Primary Education Project, 1972). They covered topics such as planning the integrated day and preparing teachers to work in such schools.

About half the monographs dealt with the place of the specific subjects. In a Brunerian educational world, we knew that a primary question posed to those who were attracted to such forms of education would be about subject-by-subject learning. There were special monographs on mathematics, language, science, art, music, and movement, among others, almost all of them written by educators from England. The message was that subject learning could be rich and deep in informal classrooms where subject matter was taught in connection with studying community-based problems.

The integrated day did not spread very much or survive very long, either in England or the United States. One of many reasons in the United States may have been the reluctance of its prime movers to subject their initiatives to careful scrutiny. Evaluation, even justification, was anathema. The Ford Foundation program officer in charge of the work on English infant schools, Marjorie Martus, asked me to host a meeting of Americans closely associated with the movement. The idea was to help crystallize and promote it. I was dean of the University of Illinois College of Education by then and convened the meeting at a retreat-like mansion about 25 miles from Champaign-Urbana owned by the university. About two dozen people came, including education writers who were known to be sympathetic.

The conversation was not congenial. When some of those who had established integrated-day-type schools were queried about student learning by the journalists or others in the group, they became defensive and even angry about what they seemed to think only they could really understand. Some of them acted as though their basic beliefs were being questioned when asked for details or rationale. They pointedly expressed a lack of confidence that even a basically supportive and carefully invited group could really appreciate what they were doing. Unlike the spirit of the

Plowden Report, all questions about indicators of success were resisted. The experience proved profoundly disappointing to almost everyone, not least the Ford Foundation. For me, it highlighted further the fact that evaluation of new programs was seen as a threat to many educational innovators, a matter to which we return in chapter 5 on assessment and evaluation.

California Tries Cross-Cutting Themes: Searching for the Science Content

Another opportunity to learn more systematically about subject boundaries and the issues associated with them arose in connection with the OECD studies. One of my responsibilities was to help select the American cases, then work directly on two of them. One of the latter was centered on the 1990 guidelines (called a "framework") for science education in California (California Department of Education, 1990) and how it was used. A central feature of the framework was its emphasis on *themes* that cut across the separate subject fields in science. Specific science concepts were identified within conventional subject classifications such as biological and physical sciences, but the Introduction stressed that certain themes that characterized almost all of science crossed the separate disciplinary boundaries. Six examples of such cross-disciplinary themes were mentioned in the framework: systems and interactions, patterns of change, energy, evolution, scale and structure, and stability. The accompanying statement tried to make clear that these possibilities were illustrative only, that others could be used to make the point with students that several overarching conceptions characterized and transcended the separate disciplines. These themes constituted a unifying feature; science was more than the sum of its constitutive disciplines.

The California initiative was buttressed by and integrated into a secondary school science project launched by the National Science Teachers Association (NSTA) called Scope, Sequence, and Coordination (SS&C). The executive director of NSTA at the time was highly critical of the "layer cake" approach to structuring science education at the secondary level, by which general science or earth sciences came first for a year, followed by biology, followed by chemistry, and finally finishing with physics at the "top." One reason for his critique was that many students took no more than the two years of science required for a high school diploma in most states, and so missed physics (and sometimes chemistry) entirely. Another was that students educated in such a structure had little understanding of science as a conceptually interconnected field in which the separate disciplines relate to one another in significant ways.

SS&C secured financial support for many years from the National Science Foundation to encourage the development of "integrated" or "coordinated" science. The California group responsible for promulgating framework-consistent changes in the schools formed an alliance with the NSTA. Funds were provided to the state to help high school science teachers develop courses that crossed the disciplinary boundaries. The main strategy was to bring teachers together on a regular basis to discuss their attempts to reach the thematic understandings promoted in the framework and the cross-disciplinary approaches advocated by SS&C.

New course sequences were designed. Biology, chemistry, and physics disappeared as separate subjects in many high schools; the sequence was now called Integrated Science I, Integrated Science II, Integrated Science III, and Integrated Science IV. New books were written and published to correspond with the state-approved conception.

The resulting courses, however, hardly ever attempted to underscore the deep connections among the sciences that some proponents of integrated science advocated. More frequently, they juxtaposed certain topics in a "coordinated" fashion. Students would learn that certain organisms respond to light in a characteristic manner in a chapter devoted almost exclusively to biological principles. The next chapter might center on physics, with references to how light is transmitted. Elsewhere in this chapter, Paul suggests that such an outcome may be more justifiable conceptually than the integrated approach. The California experience suggests that it seems to be more realistic.

With regard to the themes emphasized in the framework, an examination of the books and courses suggests that many of them were indeed highlighted from time to time in the new approaches. Typically, they were introduced within sections on chemistry, biology, earth sciences, and physics, however, rather than being featured as organizing principles: "coordination" again.

Themes in the Elementary School

The fate of the framework's themes at the elementary school level was particularly disconcerting to the framers. Though the six listed in the framework were suggestive only, many elementary school teachers took the notion to mean that relevant content might be clustered around interesting subject matter. "Themes" became "topics." Thus children eight years old might study whales for a few weeks. In this connection, they would read stories about whales, learn about whales in the economy, sing whaling songs, learn about whale hunting and conservation, and draw pictures of different kinds of whales. The science would consist of learning something about the whale as an organism: It is a mammal; different whales have different diets; they migrate along the California coast and give birth to their young in Mexican waters. This curriculum may appeal to third graders, but it was far from the framework authors' view of themes as transcending scientific concepts.

Stanford's Experiment in Boundary-Crossing

It is not only at elementary and high school levels that educators have embarked on a quest for teaching about the underlying principles that undergird the sciences. The challenge of designing an appropriate "general education" offering in science has long been a topic of education policy deliberations in American colleges and universities. American higher education, unlike education in many other parts of the world, aims to provide students with a broad education in the "liberal arts and sciences," as well as in a specialty. What science should be taught to those students who do not intend to major in a scientific field?

Conventionally, there are two approaches. In one, survey courses are offered, perhaps one in biological sciences and one in physical sciences. Each non-science major takes the sequence. Major concepts in the respective fields are highlighted. Usually there is a laboratory component as well. In the other approach, students are able to choose the introductory courses in any of several sciences. Those electing such programs to meet their science requirement enroll in the same courses as beginning majors in the respective disciplines, and that is their sole science requirement.

To many, neither of the two major approaches to education in science for the non-scientist is satisfactory. The survey course covers a large amount of content, but superficially. Complex topics in biology such as transmission of genetic material and ecology, for example, take about three or four weeks each. The tendency is to expect familiarity with a range of specific facts and principles, but with little understanding of the evidence for the concepts that are emphasized. The educational value of such courses is all the more questionable because the drive for coverage does little to equip the student to sustain even a spectator view of scientific developments, much less understand how science may relate to the life of any citizen in a scientific and technical age. Examinations typically do little to elicit knowledge of how the concepts are used or how they relate to other fields of science.

The introductory courses for majors in a field are seldom more satisfactory for purposes of general education. By definition, such courses attract those students with specialized interest in the subject. The pace is quick. There usually is no attempt to relate the science either to important everyday applications or even to other sciences. The disciplines taught in colleges and universities were created to facilitate understanding within compartmentalized fields. While scientists increasingly are finding links among the separate disciplines, there is usually little recognition of this fact in introductory courses. The assumption seems to be that the study of important interrelationships comes later; first it is necessary to learn the "fundamentals" within each discipline.

At Stanford, a group of about 20 science, mathematics, and engineering professors launched a new course in the late 1990s for students who are not majors in these fields that would focus on links among these disciplines. The idea was to offer an option for the students that would make it possible for them to meet graduation requirements in a specially designed program distinct from the standard introductory courses in selected disciplines. The new core would emphasize interrelationships among science, mathematics, and engineering by focusing on topics that draw content from all three fields. It was thought a thematic focus would hold students' interests and at the same time teach them the basic science concepts that characterize a rigorous general education. The NSF provided financial support.

As a result of faculty interest and subsequent deliberation, the heart was chosen as one focus. Light was another. Each student chose one of the foci, which was then pursued for the entire year. Thus a student choosing the heart learned some of the relevant biology from faculty in the Department of Biology and the School of Medicine. Physics (of fluids, for example) was taught by physics professors. Engineering and mathematics faculty taught about diagnostic and therapeutic devices for identifying and treating a range of circulatory anomalies. Analogous approaches were taken to integrating concepts from all three fields for the students who focused on the topic of light for the year. Extensive laboratory exercises were incorporated into each of the sequences, requiring further commitment of time by the faculty who chose to become involved. Not only was a large amount of planning time necessary to integrate the content, each of the professors in the early years of the Science, Mathematics, and Engineering Core Sequence (SME) decided it was necessary to sit in on the class sessions even when it wasn't apparent that their own expertise would be needed.

By the third year of the experiment, however, the number of students choosing the new sequence dropped significantly. The reasons are not entirely clear. One, apparently, was that the students did not always know what to expect. Guidelines were developed as the course progressed. Because the course had little history, there were few reliable indicators about the merits and shortcomings of the experimental sequences.

Another Reason for Boundary Breaching: Practical Work

The OECD study that focused on innovations in science, mathematics, and technology education created an opportunity to examine how other countries envisioned the relationships among these three fields in their new educational programs. Specifically, how did the curriculum developers see the connection between science and technology? Science, to simplify only slightly, represents an attempt to understand how the world works, regardless of practical utility. Technology aims to have a practical impact on human affairs.

Clearly the two enterprises, science and technology, are not identical, though they are often interconnected. The great achievements of science for the last 400 years have been associated with identifying fundamental principles with extraordinary explanatory power: gravitation, the laws of motion, transmission of genetic material, evolution (of biological organisms and the physical universe), and plate tectonics. Technology, broadly defined, is about designing objects and/or procedures to change the ways in which people get things done. Often technology stems from science: Understanding the nature of the electromagnetic field led to development of methods of generating electric power. Frequently, however, people figure out the technology before the scientific theory is developed: Aqueducts to transport water were built almost two millennia before the physical principles that made them possible were understood. Historically, in fact, science is often stimulated by the innovations of people who try to solve real-world problems. Germ theory was developed decades after a Viennese physician, Ignaz Semmelweis, demonstrated that complications associated with childbirth could be reduced dramatically if doctors washed their hands before assisting mothers to deliver their babies. Semmelweis had been stimulated to introduce this procedure in his hospital when he noticed that babies born at home faced fewer life-threatening risks than those born in the hospital. While conditions at home were not always sanitary, doctors in hospitals typically shuttled directly between sick people and the mother in labor. The technology of hand-washing had dramatic and immediate effects on infant mortality, and helped to stimulate scientific research about the underlying reasons.

Technology as a New Subject

A pervasive trend in the countries that participated in the OECD study was a move toward more practical work. The most dramatic manifestation was creation of a new and separate subject, technology. Practical work, often emphasizing applications of science, was being introduced to heighten students' interest in science. It is a fact, at least in American schools, that only a small percentage of students choose to specialize in science. But if science is an important element in the education of all children, its study might be more compelling for the majority if it were related to things they care about and encounter on a regular basis. When their school subjects become more relevant to the lives of the students, however, the individual disciplines prove to be inadequate. To develop a policy about amelioration of the damage done by earthquakes, it is necessary to understand how and where earthquakes are most likely to occur. Such knowledge comes from geological studies of plate tectonics, the characteristics of different types of fault lines, and patterns of seismic activity around the globe—clearly realms of science. But it also requires knowledge of different building materials and their responses to stress, the kinds of preparations that can be made for people to survive after a seismic disaster, and a familiarity with risk factors at a neighborhood-by-neighborhood level. Design of appropriate structures and related building codes, in turn, depend on highly localized rock and soil conditions.

Not least, earthquake preparedness and survivability is related to policies and practices with respect to routing traffic and telephone calls, storing food for emergency purposes individually and in the community, disaster reaction procedures by public service agencies like police and fire departments, and much more. No single field of science is enough to comprehend most practical issues. The trend toward more practical work we found in every country involved in the OECD study was one more justification (and source of pressure) for blurring the boundaries among the separate sciences; between science and mathematics; and even between science and mathematics, on the one hand, and matters of feasibility, cost, community priorities, and political support, on the other.

A Developmental View of Boundaries: Some Half-Baked Theorizing

Much of my classroom teaching career was at the elementary school level. One reason that I shifted away from secondary schools was that I found younger children somewhat more overtly curious about phenomena around them and spontaneous than those who were older. Preadolescents seemed more transparent and straightforward than the students I taught in high schools. Seven-year-old boys and girls, I noticed repeatedly, could spend an hour or more trying to figure out the relationship among the length of a pendulum, its mass, and its periodicity. Provided with a string and several bobs, they measured, weighed, and timed. They discussed ways of improving their accuracy when repeated observations yielded somewhat different results. Sometimes they even decided to calculate averages for several of their observations—and made rough but effective estimates of how to do it—even though they hadn't been learning much more than simple addition and subtraction in their arithmetic classes.

There was no obvious use for the science they were learning, no ready application of the principles involved. They hardly ever asked what a pendulum is used for, or why the relationships among mass, length, and periodicity that caught their attention are important. They seemed interested in the phenomenon itself—for the sheer pleasure, apparently, of figuring out how something works. Furthermore, the children seemed content to continue the pendulum investigation for much longer periods than the "limited attention span" many experts on the development of young children attributed to seven-year-olds. And they displayed similar levels of curiosity and persistence in figuring out how certain insect larvae move up (or down) slopes of different angles, how these organisms react to light, and whether or not they move toward water. Their inherent interest in many natural objects and events carried them into realms of scientific investigation that few adults expected or imagined, regardless of connections with anything else in their lives.

Not so older children, those about 12 or 13, at least not commonly, and not in my experience. They are even less likely to be spontaneous (at least with respect to subject matter) in the presence of other children their own age—as, for example, in a classroom where the teacher is trying to teach science. Older children, in my experience, often assume an attitude of indifference. Sometimes the resistance is overt. "So what?" ask a few. "Why do we have to study this?" "Will it be on the test?" These were often the very same children who, a few years earlier, were delighted to design scientific investigations for the joy and satisfaction of the activity itself.

Whatever the reasons for the attitudinal shift, it seemed to me unmistakable and consistent: Early adolescents seemed less willing to study science for its own sake than those who were younger. If so, one curriculum implication may be that those secondary school students not already predisposed to continue with science need additional reasons for pursuing the subject if educational policymakers insist that all students should study science for a specified number of years. How does science relate to them personally? Is knowledge of science necessary to lead a healthy life? What impact does knowledge of science have on the community? Is science knowledge essential to earning a satisfying livelihood?

This line of reasoning, however implicit, may be one factor propelling the move toward more practical work that we found throughout the OECD research. An emphasis on connections between science and the real world is necessary to engage most students of secondary school age in the subject. On the other hand, the curriculum for younger children can be more open to the possibility of teaching science for its own inherent worth and the pleasure it accords.

PAUL'S STORIES

Integrated Science or Coordinated Sciences?

I have only once given a conference address and had some acquaintances of long standing come up to me at the end and express dismay at what I had been saying. The occasion was the 1986 annual January meeting of the Association for Science Education (ASE). This remarkably strong association of school science teachers in the United Kingdom had appointed me their honorary president for the year, and one duty that went with this honour was to give a presidential address. I chose to talk about the links between the separate science disciplines in the school curriculum. The burden of my talk was that the concept of integrated science was a confused and unsound basis for attempts to meet the need to coordinate science teaching (Black, 1986). It was not surprising that those who had invested a great deal in fostering this concept were upset.

When I first became director of the Chelsea Centre for Science Education, a constituent college of the University of London, I had leadership responsibility in research and curriculum development work across the sciences, which in school science in the United Kingdom at that time meant in biology, chemistry, and physics. Amongst the projects based in the Centre was one on the aftercare and dissemination of an integrated science project. Lectures that I had heard by that project's leaders had left me uneasy about their rationale for the course, and when I found that a chapter in their school texts entitled "Particles" tried to treat electrons and living cells in one unified presentation I became very uneasy. Nevertheless, some of the material was excellent. The project had attracted strong commitment from those who taught it, but these enthusiasts had suffered in notable battles when parents in their schools, being dismayed to learn that their children would gain school leaving certificates in "Science" and not in identifiable sciences such as "Physics," conducted campaigns to force the schools to drop the project and revert to teaching the separate sciences.

I chose to devote my presidential address to the issues involved because I saw the occasion as an opportunity to raise the matters that troubled me. My main thesis was that were strong reasons for replacing the current practice of teaching the separate sciences as independent and more or less isolated subjects by a coordinated approach, but that the integrated science movement had created an ersatz unity that ignored significant differences between the philosophies, epistemologies, and practices of the different sciences. It seemed to me that a dangerous justification for this unity would be a thoroughgoing reductionist view, in which all science would be seen to derive from physics. Then one would not stop at the boundary of biology. The social sciences would wait to be colonised also. I could not accept these implications. Of course, there are overlaps between, say, chemistry and biology, so the boundary between them is a fuzzy one, but the fact that a boundary is fuzzy rather than precise does not mean that the two bordering countries are a single country.

My argument was supported in part by my perception that the conceptually weak aspects of the otherwise excellent Integrated Science project lay precisely in those aspects in which the course tried to create integrating concepts. I was also influenced by my acquaintance with research projects in cross-disciplinary problems: An ecologist working on problems of pollution had expressed the opinion that the best way to build a strong team was to bring together experts in the separate disciplines of chemistry, plant biology, hydrology, soil science, and meteorology. The interplay between those with different but deep expertise would yield the best results.

However, the arguments for "coordination" as opposed to "integration" seemed to me to be very strong. I was aware that where three science subjects were taught separately, pupils often encountered common concepts, notably energy, in three different ways, so that what could have been a fruitful unity became at best a divided trio, and at worst a source of confusion. I had also been confronted, by my own children, with a curriculum pattern in which, for the last two or three years leading up to public certificate examinations, they had to reduce the total load of science study by dropping either one or two of the three sciences. It seemed absurd that if, for example, you were keen on physics and chemistry, your education in biology would cease at age 13.

The solution was to set up a "double-subject" coordinated science course, one that would assign the curriculum time previously taken by two of the separate sciences, would include a balanced menu across all three, and would have carefully designed cross-links among them so that a particular concept initially developed in one area would be taken up, used, and further developed in a later area using the same language and the same approach. I was able, in my capacity as advisor to the Nuffield-Chelsea Curriculum, to set up a curriculum project on this basis. We recruited an excellent trio, a biologist, a chemist, and a physicist, each with previous experience of curriculum development work and each with some experience of teaching the materials of the Integrated Science project.

The outcome of this development, the Nuffield Co-ordinated Sciences Course, achieved success in the numbers taking it up and in its wider influence. One feature of that success was that teachers who had trained in, and spent many years teaching in, one discipline were able to use the course as a vehicle to achieve a unifying approach with their colleagues without having to give up their expertise and enthusiasm for their own specialist disciplines.

However, this course was only one element in a wider movement. Apart from several competing sets of course materials for double-subject science, there had been established an ambitious Secondary Science Curriculum Review, which, with financial support from the government, was undertaking a thorough review of science teaching. Its leader, Dick West, was well aware of the struggles faced by those who had first tried to establish integrated science courses. He set up meetings with the ASE; with university departments of science, engineering, and medicine; with the Royal Society; and with employers and industry. With their public backing, he could support schools in the task of convincing parents that certificate results in (say) physics and chemistry would not be as useful to their children as double-subject science, and that a public examination certificate in this new subject would be recognised and accepted in the world outside of schools. Through West's energy and foresight the campaign achieved remarkable success.

In consequence, the group set up to advise on the science component of the new national curriculum in 1997 did not hesitate to frame the national curriculum as a coordinated course across the sciences. As described in chapter 1, that group's attempts to broaden the aims of science education failed, but they did succeed in establishing a double-subject model for all students with four components, one each in life sciences, chemistry, and physics, and a fourth in science investigations.

When I was appointed to the National Curriculum Council, a body set up to advise the government on the formulation and implementation of the national curriculum proposals, I encountered the fierce argument that these had provoked. A minority led by the elite private schools wanted to retain examinations in the separate sciences alongside the double-subject option, in part because their highly qualified teachers did not want to teach across the specialties, in part because the promise of certification in the separate sciences would enhance their special appeal to those parents who could afford their fees. Opponents like myself feared that this would lower the status of the new double-subject science and put pressure on the publicly maintained schools to imitate the elite's practices. The outcome was a compromise: Starting from the argument that an education omitting one of the three sciences was inadequate, it was agreed that a pupil could take examinations in the separate sciences provided that they were taken in all three. The tradition of dropping one and taking only two would not be supported.

A quite different argument came from those who could not accept that all pupils should be required by law to spend two subjects' worth of time on the sciences. Here were educators who did not give science education the importance that I had come to take for granted. They pleaded for the pupils who wanted to study two or three foreign languages or to continue with Latin alongside History; if science were to have its double share, they would not have time to follow their interests. Again there came a compromise. Single-subject science was to be formulated and allowed as an option, but it was to be as demanding intellectually as its double-subject counterpart. This turned out, not surprisingly, to be unrealistic.

More generally, what was striking in the National Curriculum debates about science was the almost complete absence of any broader justification for the place of science in the curriculum as a whole. From my position as chair of the assessment and testing group, I argued that those planning the mathematics science and English curricula should have an active liaison committee to look particularly at the overlaps and overloads that my group could see looming on the primary school horizon, and which would get worse as the other subjects were brought into play. This was set up, but got nowhere and was dissolved as soon as my assessment group had completed its work. There was no enthusiasm for it in the ministry, and the chair of the mathematics group was also very lukewarm. A few years later, the overload became the serious problem that we had foreseen. This, however, was only one example of a more fundamental weakness in the planning of the national curriculum, in that the separate subjects were seen as ends in themselves and not as contributors to an overall view of the learning needs of pupils. My later efforts in the National Curriculum Council to open up debate on the aims of the whole curriculum were suppressed: Ministry officials had advised the council's chairman that such academic discussions were an unwelcome diversion.

Un-Applied Mathematics

No physicist needs convincing about the importance of mathematics in science. My own experience in research was that however much mathematics you had studied, you always wished you had done more: You could never predict when a research problem would throw up a need to model situations in ways that your mathematics repertoire could not handle.

Yet in undergraduate teaching in Birmingham the physics faculty found it hard to achieve synergy between the courses taught by the mathematicians and the needs of the physics courses. It required very detailed negotiation as to timing, technical language, and symbols if the links between these courses were to be evident to students. The problems of transfer between different contexts of learning were far more difficult than we imagined: We had, after all, progressed to postdoctoral levels in physics in part because such difficulties had never bothered us. Furthermore, in both their physics and their mathematics courses, most students would be struggling at the leading edge of their growing understanding, so that in neither would they have the confidence to start working across the boundaries. The same problems arose in my work, described in chapter 2, as part of the team that was devising the new Nuffield Advanced-level Physics curriculum. Here we had to accept that the students would be taking the course in many different schools, so we could not guarantee any particular degree of collaboration between the mathematics and the physics teaching.

To tackle the difficulty we specified precisely the mathematics that the physics course would need. We also tried to develop mathematical thinking within the context of the need to model one's understanding of a physical system. Thus the concept of random decay from a collection of radioactive nuclei led to formulation of a decay law, and this could be shown to lead to the exponential function.

Another way of addressing the problem was to avoid some of the needs for the mathematics of functions by use of numerical methods for the solution of equations. Thus for a differential equation, the solutions using sophisticated functions could be bypassed by an approach in which one specified some particular starting numbers and then followed the rule expressed in the physical equation to see what would happen. This would be an incredibly slow approach with calculation by hand, but as computing equipment developed the idea became more feasible. Overall, we were not avoiding the mathematics, we were just doing them differently.

None of this was completely satisfactory. If mathematics were indeed "the handmaiden of the sciences," we ought to be able to do better than just invent pieces within a science course for students who, at the same time, were sitting in mathematics lessons where the subject looked quite different.

I tried to tackle this unease soon after I became director of the Chelsea Centre for Science Education. There were four mathematics educators on the faculty, including one full professor, so it soon made sense to change the title to "Centre for Science and Mathematics Education." I set up discussions between science educators and mathematics educators with a view to our formulating a project to "do something" about the science/mathematics interface in school learning. The mathematicians were resistant, for they had long experience of failure in trying to work on this problem area, and judged that it presented problems that were too intractable to be worth investment of effort. They felt constrained by the need to include in their curriculum some mathematics that scientists do not use. Furthermore, there was the underlying problem that cross-subject transfer was difficult because it was notoriously hard to overcome the general problem of context-bound learning. There were also problematic relationships between different subject departments in the schools: the notion of either department being the "handmaiden" of the other would be unacceptable.

More recently, the British Institute of Physics has supported a curriculum development project to renew the teaching of advanced physics to students aged 16 to 19. Those involved had to go round the same debate. One important shift in thinking was to recognise that mathematics is the language in which physicists do theory. The handmaiden notion is too ambiguous, and too limiting. It follows that if a science teaching course is to exemplify how theory is made, then the mathematics will have to be built in as the language in which such theory is spoken, not as a set of techniques borrowed from elsewhere.

It is not obvious that the mathematics–science boundary is of the same character as the intersciences boundary discussed in the previous section. For example, whilst the results of the physicist may constitute a starting basis for the work of a chemist, mathematics is more than this to the theoretical scientist, who is as likely as not to develop new mathematics in the course of trying to work through the implications of a new way of constructing a theoretical model. At the same time, pure mathematics has its own distinctive perspectives and values, and is not to be subsumed into the territory of the sciences, and indeed is as different from them as the study of history is from either area.

Technology: Not the Application of Science?

Technology was a topic on the far horizon of my concerns until two people told me that I should engage with it. One of these was my predecessor in my chair at Chelsea, Kevin Keohane. Apart from the fact that he was an old friend, I also had to take his view seriously because he was chair of the Nuffield-Chelsea Curriculum Trust, for which I was the educational consultant. The other person was Charles Phelps, recently appointed principal of Chelsea College. It would have been hard to resist either one of these, impossible to resist both.

I was aware that there was much activity in the field of teaching technology in school, but confused as to any clear basis for defining the subject, let alone relating it to science. This called for indulgence from a think tank and the Nuffield-Chelsea Trust provided the resources to set this up. Nine people agreed to come together for this purpose, meeting at the only times they could all be free, which were a set of Saturday mornings at intervals of about a month, for about a year. An important decision was that the exercise had to be jointly led by someone prominent in technology education in partnership with myself. When the obvious person, Geoffrey Harrison, then a professor at Nottingham Polytechnic, agreed, we had a good basis, further strengthened by the fact that we were able to develop a close working relationship.

The outcome was a booklet entitled *In Place of Confusion* (Black & Harrison, 1985), which commanded attention in the field for the next few years. One main message was to reject the view that technology is merely the application of science. The definition of technology, central to the whole argument, was that it is the application of a diverse variety of resources to meet human needs. The knowledge, skills, and methods of science provided an important set of potential resources, but the resources needed in any particular technological enterprise might also include ideas derived from mathematics, the social sciences, language and media presentation studies, and the techniques of brainstorming. The "problem" of the technologist was different in character from the "problem" of the scientist.

The curriculum implications were more far-reaching than I had anticipated. Given the concept that the group formulated, it followed that technology in the school ought to have two distinctive characteristics. The first was made clear by the British Royal Society of Arts, which had issued a manifesto about the need for education in what they called "capability." Their reasoning was that most of the school curriculum was about passive study. It would develop the critic, the wise observer, the administrator; it would not encourage the creative, the entrepreneur, the maker and marketer of goods and services. So we argued for pupils' learning to be focused on real and practical creative projects in order to give priority to education in capability.

The second implication was that school technology ought to be a cross-curricular subject, so operated in the school that ideas from all parts of the curriculum might be drawn in and used. In this view, the curriculum could be seen as the interplay between interdisciplinary *task areas*, of which technology was one, and *resource areas*, which would comprise most of the traditional school disciplines. Without pupil involvement in task areas, education for capability would not be achieved. Clearly this vision would call for new approaches to curriculum planning, and it implied a formidable agenda for action.

There followed a series of initiatives in which Geoffrey Harrison and I collaborated, funded at first by the oil firm British Petroleum and later by the government Department of Trade and Industry. The rewards came in the work we were able to do with schools, which we eventually reported in a book for which most of the chapters were written by different teachers describing the various ways in which they had implemented cross-curricular arrangements for promoting student work on the tackling of realistic problems (Murray, 1990). Some set up an end-on arrangement, pursuing a task in the lessons of one subject up to a certain point, and then handing on the work to the lessons of another subject. Others arranged that all the timetable time of two or three school subjects would be devoted to the same piece of work for about three weeks, giving pupils an opportunity to concentrate at the rate of about nine school periods a week guided by different teachers from period to period. An example was a study of the dangers of hypothermia in older people living alone and unable to afford proper heating. Some pupils worked on electronic warning systems, some on appropriate and inexpensive diets, some on cheap insulating materials, whilst guidance from social science and English teachers led to a set of interviews with older people about their opinions. The interviews showed that some of the technical solutions were unacceptable. An example was rejection of an arrangement that flashed a light outside one's door when the temperature inside was too low: People did not want such a public advertisement of their poverty.

Most radical of all was the school that suspended the entire timetable for two weeks so that they could work full-time on a collective basis. One year the project was to select an Olympic sport and design a suitable stadium to be located in their town with good transport to the local city, Manchester, which was actively committed to bidding to be the next Olympics venue. The teachers involved stressed that they were resource persons, to be called upon to help answer questions and provide guidance; the direction of the project was in the hands of the students. Their project's results were presented to the real Olympic bid committee, which came to the school in response to an invitation and thereby engendered local media publicity.

What was remarkable in these several initiatives was the commitment and unexpected talents that were evoked from the pupils, to the surprise of their teachers and of ourselves. A second feature was the realisation that with collaboration between its several staff a large secondary school could draw upon a wide range of resources to tackle any project, and could also draw on local community resources—particularly where the project had appeal because it was a realistic task rather than an academic "school" exercise. It seemed sad that the potential for education that these findings revealed was not being exploited in most schools.

The territory of school technology had long been a field of contention in many countries. Some saw it as part of the science curriculum. Teachers of metalwork and woodwork saw it as an extension of their craftwork, for by adding some work on plastics and some attention to design skills they could enhance the low status of their work under a new title, Technology. Others again emphasised that design ought to be the leading and unifying concept. In other countries it has been tied to folkcraft traditions (Scandinavia), or to training in industrial production (Communist East Germany) (Layton, 1990). When the new National Curriculum was set up, the inclusion of technology as a required subject set the scene for a fierce debate.

The outcome was the establishment of a new subject, called Design and Technology (Black, 1991). It was meant to embrace the existing school subjects of Art and Design, Home Economics (which included work on food, clothing, furnishing, and home management), the Crafts in metals, wood, and plastics, Business Studies, and any combination of these currently using the title Technology. It was definitely not a part of science. The unifying theme was the definition of technology as a way of meeting human needs by calling on a wide variety of resources. The learning envisaged was to be centred on students' experience in tackling a carefully articulated menu of realistic projects.

The implementation led to much confusion and distress among teachers (Paechter, 2000). There were managerial stresses in bringing together teachers who had previously worked separately using different models of teaching and learning. Other challenges were pedagogical in developing new ways of giving students independence and in designing and tackling their own solutions to problems, whilst giving careful guidance to help achieve the learning, as needs arose, of appropriate knowledge and skills so that the products would be of good quality. The evaluation of the first years of implementation reported concern about poor quality: pupils had freedom without help, so the products too often used cardboard and sticky tape. Clearly teachers needed more help and support, and concern about this need led to the work already described in chapter 2 on the development of new curriculum materials.

What was lost in an otherwise remarkable new curriculum achievement was the cross-curricular potential of the subject. Teachers were under so much pressure with the onset of the national curriculum and assessment that there was no energy left to engage in intersubject innovations; those thrown together to make the new subject work had enough problems to tackle as they tried to work among themselves.

Reflecting on this technology story, it first becomes clear that the boundary between science and technology is different again in character from the boundaries between the sciences or between science and mathematics. Both philosophically and practically, human technology involves far more than the application of science. In order to be practical, science knowledge has to be transformed—reformulated in terms that meet the exigencies of particular applications, and then constrained and oriented within a needs context that reconciles a set of competing priorities. The achievements of science are a contribution, one amongst many, to a different, arguably more significant and more complex enterprise.

When designing the supporting cables for a suspension bridge, the engineer needs to know the cost, strength, corrosion resistance, and fatigue resistance of the alternative materials available; (s)he does not normally need to explore the atomic theory of elasticity or of surface chemistry, but (s)he does need to optimise the choice of material for the particular context, for example corrosion may be very important close to industrial centres, less so in open country.

It follows that for science education to claim ownership of technology education, or even to claim primus inter pares in a collaborative approach to technology, is not a defensible or practically useful posture. Thus, the movements in many countries that, created as developments of science education, march under the banner of Science, Technology, and Society seem problematic. They have broken some of the constraints that had kept the science curriculum too austerely pure, but in some cases they have also led science educators into colonising a territory to which they should really only lay claim as partners with others.

In an evaluation study for a technology innovation, David Layton described a class in which pupils were arguing whether or not a particular technological change should, in the light of its effects on the environment, be allowed to proceed. Teachers from several school departments observed the to and fro of heated arguments among the pupils. Afterward, the science and the craft teachers thought that the discussion had been pointless: Nothing had been decided, the argument had gone nowhere. The humanities teachers, however, saw it as excellent education: Pupils had had their ideas challenged, had been forced to reexamine their assumptions, and had learnt that views opposed to their own could be argued with as much cogency as they themselves could muster. So one group of teachers would not value such an event, whilst the other would see it as central. Who should have power to guide the learning about values that ought to be an essential part of the agenda of any education in technology? More generally, could these teachers ever share an overall view of the aims of education in the light of which they might reevaluate the contributions of their own subjects?

JOINT REFLECTIONS ABOUT BOUNDARIES

We both have learned and taught within the boundaries of the separate science subjects, and we both have encountered attempts to abolish those boundaries. As we have seen these two approaches play out during our careers, both can be educationally attractive, but both can also be sterile. Many attempts to cross disciplinary boundaries have been superficial. On the other hand, a specific science discipline taught with little attention to connections with other ways of understanding the world can be artificial and remote.

Our Conclusions

We are both inclined toward a curriculum that establishes connections between science and the world outside the classroom relatively early in a student's studies. It is true that many primary school children are happily absorbed in learning science for its own sake. But most students, particularly as they approach adolescence, seem to crave explicit connections between life in school and the reality of the adult world. Cross-curricular perspectives try to mirror real-world complexities. They call for resources that no one subject can provide. At they same time, they can be practical, and—insofar as they are projects within a local community—some can even *be* reality, rather than surrogates. Current theories of learning emphasize the importance of activities that are complex and realistic, for they test and enhance crucially important features of a student's knowledge and help to develop both the structure and the flexibility that can grow through tackling the challenges of real applications.

Therefore, a desirable goal would be a curriculum that moves back and forth between engendering deep understanding of scientific phenomena and introducing some of the challenges and complexities of relating scientific knowledge to real-world issues. Using both approaches holds the greatest promise of sustaining interest over time for the broadest range of students.

In the end, it seems to us that the school should mirror the world of science itself, which is one of separate communities of practice, yes, but also one in which communities interact and borrow across their boundaries, move the fences whenever it seems convenient, and create new enclaves for new communities whenever practice requires stronger relationships. Boundaries don't necessarily imprison if one is alert for opportunities to transcend them.

A key issue in designing the science curriculum, and a major threat to the quality of any orientation toward science, is the pressure for coverage. Whatever the mix of approaches to the subject, the biggest error would be to try to address too many discrete topics, either within a discipline or in examining how they relate to one another in addressing practical issues. Whether science is taught on a disciplinary or cross-disciplinary basis, the greatest threat to quality is superficiality. Unfortunately, the threat is real. Most textbooks and curricula put the emphasis on the number of topics that are included rather than the soundness of how each one is treated. Examinations often exacerbate the problem. Many teachers, through predilection or pressure, skim the surface of the subject.

Our main point, however, is that decisions about design of the science program should be set in the context of more comprehensive considerations about the curriculum as a whole. What is it designed to do? What coverage makes sense? How do the various subjects contribute to desired educational ends, alone or in concert? Hardly any of the major thoughts about the science curriculum raise questions about the context and assumptions about the curriculum as a whole. It is certainly conceivable that science educators may be attempting to meet needs that would be far better met by others if the curriculum were examined seriously in its entirety.

4

Pedagogy and Learning

New styles of teaching have emerged over the decades. The recitation still dominates the field of science instruction, as it does for most subjects. The teacher exposits, then asks questions, then seeks responses, preferably in the words of the text. More varied pedagogical repertoires are regularly advocated and are beginning to take root, however. These can be characterized as a broad and slow trend toward the teacher increasingly assuming the role of facilitator of student learning. No one can learn for someone else, so the teacher creates an environment in which students are able to advance their own knowledge. What are those optimal settings that strengthen the student's inclination and ability to learn something of importance? How does the teacher help create them?

One hears the metaphor of guide or coach to describe some of these approaches. Increasingly this style of teaching employs the use of small groups of students working together to complete a task or project. A considerable amount of research in psychology and sociology supports these pedagogical approaches. Introducing them in more classrooms, however, is far from simple. Change for anyone is scary. It might also be risky because a different kind of relationship is necessary between teacher and student and among teachers, students, and parents.

MIKE'S STORIES

Problem Solving in the Community

My interests in enlisting students as active participants in their own learning date from my doctoral studies and dissertation. Dewey, as I indicated in chapter 1, was a strong influence on me with his view of problem solving as the core of scientific method and also for his emphasis on studies of the student's own community. I was drawn also to the work of Gestalt psychologist Max Wertheimer (1945), who was delving into problem solving itself. Problem-solving approaches were also being legitimated in educational practice through an ascending postwar educational ideology and philosophy that had begun to take shape in the 1930s and that posited that the best education was one in which students became deeply involved in exploring their own environments. Schools do not exist solely to prepare students for their lives as adults. Rather, they are also places where young people engage in meaningful activities at their own level. The teacher is the person who guides that activity in the light of her grasp of the fields of human knowledge that are available. The personal and social relevance of the knowledge enhances student motivation, makes it easier to retain, and connects life in school with the world outside.

Fortunately for my own evolving educational philosophy, this general approach to teaching and learning was promoted in Great Neck, New York, from 1950–1955 when I taught there. For the most part, the teachers in the schools in which I worked shared an educational viewpoint that emphasized socially and personally relevant knowledge. Consistent with that view, the Great Neck schools at that time placed the classroom teacher in the position of authority and responsibility for the entire program for the children in her class. The story of my work with Marion Billhardt in chapter 1 epitomizes the approach. People like me with subject specialization could advise and assist, but it was the teacher who met with the students all day who was the final arbiter of what happened in her classroom. My ministrations were suggestive only. It was a point of view I came to respect and value, sensing that teaching is highly personal and not easily or quickly modified by outside influences, a point to which we will return.

Group Work

It was during these years that I became personally acquainted for the first time with a particular pedagogical technique that I began to see often and that seemed appealing: Organizing classes in small groups so that children could collaborate in their efforts to learn. I am unable to recall a single instance in my own elementary or secondary education in which a primary method of acquiring essential academic content entailed organizing the larger class in such a manner. Group activity was for the playground, extracurricular pursuits (interest-based clubs sponsored by the school, for example), or subjects that were not considered academic, such as drama or large-scale artwork. Even in science labs in high school, we almost always worked alone—which usually did not stop us, of course, from trying to get help from classmates who seemed more knowledgeable. Nor was small-group activity a feature of the high school in which I taught for two years before deciding to teach younger children.

The Great Neck curriculum was different. For most grades, it was organized into "units," thematic segments that usually lasted from three to eight weeks and that consumed virtually all the class time during that period. A common focus for the entire third-grade year was a study of the local community. One aspect of this study was almost always a unit that might last for two months on various community services. The teacher would often begin the unit by asking the children to think about and list the various agencies that had been established for safety, education, provision of utilities, and the like. The students proceeded to list police and fire departments, libraries, and schools. They added such functions as garbage collection and disposal, water and power provision, and medical services as they warmed to the possibilities and received prompts from the teacher. During this time, the students usually worked as an entire class. In a few classrooms, small groups of four or five children worked together to generate the lists.

Then the teacher, most commonly working with the entire class, would move into a phase in which the students would begin formulating questions they would like to investigate about the various services: What are the crime rates in the community? What are the most common crimes? What are the schedules of the police? How are they determined? How does the community figure out where to place fire stations and hydrants? How long does it take for emergency services to respond in different sections of the town? Are there differences? Why? How is the water supply kept clean? How are funds raised to support the range of community services? Who decides how much should be spent? Encouraged by the teacher, the children easily generated lists of 30 or 40 questions. At this stage, the teacher placed them on the chalkboard, unedited except for clarification.

At some time later that day or the next, after the questions had been displayed for students to think about, the teacher typically reconvened the class to study the list. Which ones seemed to be repetitions? Which questions related to one another? Which ones seemed most important? As she aimed for relevance, congruence, and saliency, she became more a contributor to the group's discussion than she had been while the list was generated. Her aim was to pare down the list to the most important questions, but with an eye also toward grouping them in some coherent and logical fashion, so that subsequently the students could work collaboratively in small groups to pursue their investigations of the questions they had formulated. One group might study police services, another fire, another the town government and its structure.

This was where I came in. If a group became involved in fire safety and wanted to study fire-retardant materials, the teacher might arrange for me to meet with that group of children (which we typically called a "committee") to help them organize their study and obtain material for experiments and demonstrations. Or the group working on water supply might want to learn about water purification, so I would help them locate relevant materials. A group studying health services might want to learn about immunization practices.

There was no single science textbook that laid out the third-grade science curriculum. I had files full of material—pamphlets, newspaper clippings, magazine articles, and the like—on various topics for use by the students, and usually knew how to obtain more. The school library had other resources. I helped the students identify relevant materials as they delved into their questions. As part of my responsibility for improving science teaching in the district, I spent about a quarter of my time working with students in small groups who were engaged in investigations about questions that their class had determined to be important in connection with a larger study.

As my career carried me away from Great Neck and into many more classrooms, I came to see this style of teaching advocated widely, but not extensively practiced. Where I did see it, students assumed responsibility for much of their learning, with the teacher designing the conditions under which such learning might best occur. She would teach entire classes of students directly, of course, but the pedagogical repertoire of these elementary school teachers was broad. They often split their time among the small groups. Teachers organized their work so that they could meet individually with a child during class time while other students were engaged in group work. The students in such classes seemed significantly more engaged in their studies than in classes where there was more dependence on the teacher. I believe the children learned more, too.

Discovery or Invention: A Foray into Learning Theory

During this period, and consonant with it, I began to hear and see more about teaching by "discovery." As students became involved directly in science-based investigations about the world around them, it was not unusual for some teachers, in fact, to adopt a solely facilitative role. That is, they seemed to believe that it was necessary only to create settings in which students could conduct investigations, and the students would then learn the desired science. They made the assumption that the students could arrive at some of the major intellectual understandings that characterize modern science by their independent efforts alone. It began to dawn on me that while it made good sense to engage students as active participants in their own learning, it was overly optimistic to expect them to generate the profound insights of a Kepler, Koch, or Newton. Of course, I don't suppose many teachers attracted to discovery methods expected that, either, but their teaching sometimes seemed to me to be based on such an assumption. They were either unwilling to play a strong role in leading students to modern scientific concepts, or they did not believe that learning those concepts were a priority, or they did not feel competent to discuss the relevant science—or they were much more patient than I.

I was involved by that time in the astronomy project, where we were devoting considerable effort to identifying key ideas in astronomy for students to study. The task was intellectually challenging. Obviously we thought the matter important, even central, so it seemed important to me for the teacher to take a stronger role in creating the general intellectual framework in which modern ideas could be probed and better understood. Content is important, even for elementary school grades, I believed. I started to raise questions about the exclusive use of teaching primarily by discovery. At about this time, I decided to take the sabbatical leave at the University of California, Berkeley, to spend a year with Robert Karplus. (He was, in 1960, a physics professor who was the recipient of the other NSF curriculum development grant below the high school level.) Karplus and his colleagues were trying to figure out how to help primary school children understand fundamental physical concepts such as frames of reference (how the motion of objects appears from different vantage points) and magnetic fields. How might fundamental principles of physics like these be taught to second graders?

Karplus appreciated the importance of engaging children in first hand attempts to understand the world, but, like me, he cared deeply as well about *what* they learned by such a process. He and I were convinced that certain science concepts were more powerful than others and that students do better to direct their investigations in school toward learning those ideas rather than others. We seemed to differ in this view from some other curriculum developers who were working with young children at the time, including several distinguished physicists associated with the Physical Sciences Study Committee at Cambridge, such as David Hawkins and Phil Morrison. They believed that authentic engagement of children at young ages with natural phenomena was the priority and that the precise subject matter was less important, at least in elementary schools.

Karplus and I took the view that one did not need to choose between the two. Independent discovery could be encouraged in the context of trying to comprehend scientific ideas with intellectual mileage, ideas that led to deeper understanding of some phenomenon. Teaching could and should include an active role for the teacher in leading even young students directly to certain key ideas in science. We posited that it might be useful to distinguish "invention" from "discovery." While the separation is not clear-cut, we suggested that children make inventions all the time to interpret the observations they make. They must do so to make sense of their world. Inevitably, they also make discoveries that enable them to refine the concepts they are forming. Most of these inventions and discoveries reflect a type of natural philosophy, a commonsense orientation popular in a culture at a particular time. They include what might be considered myths and/or naïve conceptions, as well as some that are consistent with currently accepted ideas. The objective of science instruction, we believed, was to help students look at natural phenomena from the distinctive vantage point of modern science. Sometimes this perspective differs from the culturally prevalent view. In general, we said, teaching programs should not be based on the expectation that children can invent the modern science concepts. Their spontaneously invented concepts present too much of a block.

Guiding Discovery

Since children are seldom able to invent the modern concept, particularly if it does not seem commonsensical, we suggested that the teacher should introduce it. The teacher, in the process, would help the children understand how the introduced concept could be used by the students to explain their observations. In an article we co-authored titled "Discovery or Invention?" (Atkin & Karplus, 1962; Atkin, 2002), we illustrated the approach with an example from a second-grade classroom in Berkeley. In this class we introduced two physical concepts: interaction at a distance and the magnetic field. Before focusing on these topics, the children had engaged in several weeks of science activity in which they were introduced to the idea of a system. They specified the objects in different systems and noted interactions among the objects. They learned that the identification of a system could be fairly arbitrary. The major guideline was that the connections among the objects be interesting.

At this point, we asked the class to look at a system consisting of two children pulling a rope from opposite ends. We asked the two to hold opposite ends of a rope and pull gently, then strongly, as the class watched. The members of the class noted interactions between each child and the rope. They also noted, of course, the interactions between the two children. Indeed, those might be the more interesting part of the child–rope–child system. We pointed out, though, that the child-child interaction was not a *direct* interaction but a *distant* one. We stressed the new terms and asked the children again to interact strongly, then weakly.

To compress the story, the children also experimented with wooden balls to which thick rubber bands were attached with thumbtacks. They discussed interactions that were strong and weak, direct and distant, as they looked at ball–rubber band, ball–thumbtack, two-thumbtack, and two-ball interactions. They also experimented with springs. We then introduced magnets. Clearly these objects interacted, but where was the direct interaction? We told the children that people prefer to think of direct interactions, though ropes and rubber bands made distant interactions possible. Was there something between the magnets to make their interactions possible? Nothing was visible. (No child in this class suggested air.) Even though the magnetic field was not mentioned by name, the children were given the crucial idea of an "it" for the distant magnetic interactions. This step constituted what we called the "invention."

The children then tried to find the "it" by feeling with their fingers. No result. They tried a wooden ruler. No apparent result. One child tried a nail. There was an immediate and visible reaction. This led to all kinds of experiments and discoveries about the properties of what we then called the magnetic "field." (Indeed, the invention of the magnetic field is not essential to describe magnetic interactions, but without it the subsequent explorations by the children would have resulted only in the discovery of additional distant interactions between the magnets and other objects.)

We suggested by these kinds of examples that discovery and invention could be used together as teaching strategies. The problems for investigation were compelling for the students, they were unmistakably engaged, they learned what we considered to be important science, but they weren't expected to duplicate major conceptual breakthroughs such as viewing certain distant interactions such as magnetism and gravitation as taking place within a field. Once the concept of a field was invented, the students could study its properties through discovery.

A Learning Cycle

Karplus took up these ideas and carried them much further to develop a model of instruction that he tested broadly and incorporated into the curriculum materials he was developing for a major project, the Science Curriculum Improvement Study (SCIS). Essentially the approach was to give students a period of exploration in which they became familiar with a particular phenomenon. They also were encouraged to discuss their observations and generate explanations. The teacher would then carefully guide the students to an articulation of the underlying concept, or state it herself. With this new intellectual framework, the students could begin to work more independently to discover new and subtler relationships and applications.

This model of teaching and learning came to be known as the Atkin-Karplus Learning Cycle. Actually, I made no contributions to the development of the concept or the theory after the conclusion of my sabbatical leave. The attribution, in fact, is somewhat ironic, inasmuch as I later developed considerable skepticism about the usefulness for education practice of models developed primarily on the basis of theories about how children learn, a point to be examined in the chapter on research.

PAUL'S STORIES

Learner, Know Thyself

I did well in school examinations, relying on hard work just before examinations to ensure a well-stocked memory. However, some of my early experiences in school were particularly fortunate in that they impelled me to learn for myself. My Latin teacher suggested I attempt classical Greek—a subject not in the usual school curriculum—as an extra subject in the first level of school-leaving examinations (known then as the School Certificate). I had about one hour a week of one-on-one instruction with him for a year, and spent many Sunday afternoons struggling, first with the alphabet, then with the grammar and vocabulary, and lastly with the "set books". Success in the Greek examination led to a brief flirtation with the prospect of specialising in the classics trio of Greek, Latin, and Roman history, but physics tempted more strongly and became the principal subject for my undergraduate study.

In the degree course, matters were a little better. I tried to reconcile the ways in which different textbooks treated the same subject. I was pleased with myself when I discerned that the optics lecturer had formulated his lectures using just two books. I took no notes in his lectures, just followed him in the textbooks, the challenge arising when his treatment moved from one book to the other and I had to close the old book and find the location in the new source. In consequence, at the end of his course I had in fact learnt almost nothing—but I was well equipped to learn the material by myself, and subsequently did so.

The third and last year of that degree course faced us with two final examination papers that were not related to any particular course, but were about any physics that a graduate ought to know. The only advice on preparation was that we should work through all the physics we had studied thus far. I constructed schemes centred around a nine-month revision schedule, with a notebook containing about 200 formulae in physics that I dipped into at random to check my capacity to explain and derive them off the cuff. There was a strong element of rote learning here, but the need for me to organise and structure my learning achieved something deeper.

Perhaps for this reason, my ideal, when I started to lecture to undergraduates six years later in my first faculty appointment in Birmingham, was the clear logical exposition. I came to embellish this with demonstrations and application stories, but clear delivery was the pedagogic core. In the small group tutorials that I also had to conduct, the model was the same, but then I was more nervous, for if the students did not bring an agenda, as was often the case, what would there be to talk about? To deal with this fear, I developed a portfolio of mini-lectures. There was a cosmetic opening to these by way of enquiry into understanding of relevant topics, but since the inquiries were about subtle points, the transition to a mini-lecture was almost inevitable. I was achieving little insight into the students' problems as learners.

In retrospect, I can see that as a bright student I had been able to work out for myself ways to achieve a strategic overview of my learning needs, which, combined with the tactical ability to learn quickly, had given me a double advantage over those who were both slower at a tactical level and, partly because of this, rather lost at the strategic. Thus, until I learnt to see that other learners had problems that I knew not of, I was sure to be a very limited teacher.

Logic Is Not Enough

New thinking was forced on me when I assumed the role of co-director of the team developing the Nuffield Advanced-level Physics curriculum. The five other members of the team were experienced in school teaching, and I soon came to have a very high regard for their insights into the essentials of good learning. One incident that stands out in memory occurred at a meeting about the teaching of electric fields at which I presented an outline paper on the conceptual issues involved and their implications for planning a logical way through the learning. One member of the team said, "That was very helpful, Paul, and gives us the clear foundation that we need. Please now keep quiet whilst we discuss how to teach it to school pupils because you do not understand how to do that." I would have been offended had the speaker, Bill Trotter, not been a thoughtful, friendly, and experienced teacher. So I swallowed hard and tried to listen. I slowly realised that although I had not been wrong in thinking that a clear and logical conceptual framework was essential in the design of teaching, it was not enough by far. Indeed, a second critical point for me arose when, after an outline for one block of the course had been agreed upon, one of the team said, "I cannot envisage what the classroom would be like. What will the teacher and students actually be doing with this stuff?" I realised both that it was a crucial question and that I had no idea how to answer it, so I listened carefully to the lively discussion that ensued.

Within our general concern for the difference between merely knowing about something and really understanding it, an important aspect was to deploy work with equipment to reveal new phenomena and to explore them in order to establish empirical relationships. The explanation of theory would follow and would thereby be seen as an answer to questions raised by the new phenomena. It followed that many of the lessons would have to be in a laboratory. The traditional divide between theory lessons and practical lessons would be dissolved, and the practical in which one followed someone else's recipe would play little part. Some misunderstood this approach to be "discovery learning," and queried whether students could solve problems that had taxed the genius of (say) Newton. We did not entertain any such fantasy: A more accurate descriptive label for the approach would be "guided heurism."

Aiming to Learn

The aims for the new Nuffield course, as already listed in chapter 1, included the two related intentions of "learning to enquire" and "learning in the future." Several avenues were explored in our attempts to take these seriously. One way was to select one topic for a student-centred treatment. The work was focused around a set of experiments, each one of which was to be undertaken by only two or three of the students, on the basis of their own reading from recommended sources. Each group then had to explain their work to the rest and discuss their results. The collection and interlinking of these presentations would build the basis for the understanding of the topic. This achieved some success, although teachers reported surprise at the amount of help their pupils needed in explaining their findings clearly to one another.

The most challenging innovation was to work directly at the aim of learning to enquire by requiring all students to carry out two investigations of problems or phenomena for which neither methods nor answers were well known, so that they had to devise the strategies and select or adapt the equipment. The intention was that each of the two exercises should take no more than about two weeks of the physics course. An initial task was to generate enough suitable ideas for such investigations. Brainstorming amongst the team and some teachers produced a starting list of about 100 ideas, and we were able to double this after a first set of trials using ideas generated in the schools. As the work developed, schools found that they no longer needed such help: Most investigations generated ideas for further investigations. To ensure that this aspect of the course was taken seriously, the second of the two investigations was assessed by the student's own teacher using criteria in a framework set up by the team with the examining board. The results of this assessment were to contribute about 15% of the marks for the external end-of-course examination.

The challenge was to ensure that teachers understood the criteria of quality for these investigations. Often, for example, an investigation would turn out to be no more than a comparison test, of the sort that might be done for a consumer magazine, showing some planning and measurement skills, but neither informed nor guided by any concepts of physics. We had to give guidance both that these had to be avoided and that a purely qualitative study with no numerical data would almost certainly fail. Over time, study of samples of work helped us to refine the criteria.

An outstanding example was an investigation of the blowing of fuses. The student had set up a circuit so that he could see on an oscilloscope the variation of current with time when an overload current was sent through a fuse wire and the wire heated up, melted, and broke contact. He looked at ways to vary this with different overload currents. He then sketched out a theory, equating the energy input to the wire from the current with its dissipation, in heating up and then melting the wire, and in losses to the surroundings. With this theory he estimated how long it should take for the wire to reach its melting point, and compared the prediction with his measurements. This had all the right qualities: It combined experimental ingenuity, careful measurement, and theoretical modeling.

The basic aim was that the student should acquire, through involvement with the investigation, some acquaintance with the nature of the work of a scientist in empirical exploration. In refining the problem, designing the approach, and collecting and analysing data, the student should be actively using physics ideas learnt in the course, and would thereby be working toward the goal of being an independent learner in the future.

They Learn by Talking

This school curriculum development work changed the outlook with which I eventually returned to undergraduate teaching. I was no longer content to deliver material across a lectern. Given a new first-year course, I planned to imitate the most striking of the courses I had experienced as an undergraduate. This was given by the head of the department to new entrants in their first term. We were overawed that this great man deigned to teach us. He started by listing several topics, which constituted about half of his course, on the blackboard. He said that these were treated in a textbook that he specified, so there was little point in his lecturing about them. He would include them in full measure in the examination. Then he devoted his lectures to topics, some close to his own research interests, chosen to bring out key ideas and methods in physics. I was enchanted, but I was also impelled to organise my own learning from the textbook.

I planned to use this approach for my new course. I selected a text and the topics to be left for the students to study on their own. This would release time for interactive dialogue in the lectures. So on my first day back as a lecturer, I faced 90 undergraduates in their first week at university. I was almost frozen with fear. My start depended on an experiment on the bench in front of me: If it did not work, my plan was in ruins. Then I was to ask the class questions about how they would explain what was happening. If nobody volunteered an answer, I would also look foolish and be unable to proceed. I had learnt, however, that I had to tolerate silence for some time.

To my relief, the experiment worked, some brave souls responded to the opening question, and we were on our way. A key feature was to ask questions in a variety of ways. One of the most successful was to propose several alternative explanations of a phenomenon, in the form of an informal multiple choice question, and then invite the students to talk with their neighbours for a few minutes about the best choice. Then votes were taken, and for each option attracting several supporters one of these was asked to explain their reasoning.

David Boud, then a student doing a Ph.D. in course evaluation, later to become a leading figure in Australia in the study of higher education, sat in on some of the lectures and talked to the students. He reported that they both loved me and hated me. They loved me because there was a buzz— the lectures were active and unpredictable. They hated me because they felt insecure afterward. It was hard to take notes in the to and fro of discussion, and many were often unclear, after the exchange of diverse explanations, as to the best conclusion, or even about the main point of the whole exercise. I had to accept that my personal satisfaction with the clarity of my resolution of the outcomes was no guarantee of understanding by the students. I had already gotten as far as giving the students sample examination questions on the material that they had to learn from the textbook alone, and first I added sample questions on the lecture topics. This forced me to make precise my vague ideas about what I actually wanted them to achieve.

Boud's feedback reported that these moves were not enough. So, with reluctance, I provided lecture notes. These had to be written after the event, because I could not predict the paths that interactive discussions would follow. I would sit down after each lecture and make a handwritten summary, of one page only, describing the work presented and the ideas explored. I felt that what I was writing down must have been glaringly obvious to anyone who had been there, but the students found the notes very helpful. I was slowly learning about the gap between the teacher and the learner, about the need for feedback, and about the particular problem that students had in grasping an adequate overview of the teaching so that they could put each bit into a meaningful context.

Tactics and Strategies: Skill-ful Metacognition

With just four of these students in my room for a one-hour tutorial per week, I tried to engage them in a formative dialogue so that I could begin to connect with their level of thinking rather than speak from my own. It was pointless merely to ask if they had any problems; the outcome was generally silence. I had to find a way to make them present something about their learning. One way was to assign to each of the four one of their lecture courses, and ask each to present, once a fortnight, a summary of the progress of the course, in the form of a block diagram, each separate topic constituting a block, with arrows to show how the different blocks were related. This seemed to me a trivial exercise, with the merit that it would help me to see what my colleagues were up to in their lectures. The results were productive of useful talk. Recognising boundaries was sometimes tricky, and then picking out the main point of each block became important, for only with such discernment could the links between blocks be made clear. My feedback could now engage with their struggles, and from these the overall architecture of each physics topic began to emerge. After a few weeks of this, I suggested that we might now drop what seemed to me to be a five-finger exercise in learning. I was surprised when the students said they wanted to go on doing it, as it was very helpful to them. Several years were to pass before, on encountering the literature on concept-mapping and metacognition, I saw why such work could be helpful in teaching students how to learn.

A different initiative opened other perspectives. I had become interested in problem solving, and judged that one of the obstacles that made our students less than effective was their lack of certain basic skills in analysing their own learning and in confronting new problems. I was able to work with a group of physics colleagues to compose a new set of seminar classes, to be called Skill Sessions, in which small groups would work, first on their own, and then through interaction amongst several groups exchanging their findings, steered by a tutor. The work specified consisted of quite short problems designed to help focus on specific skills. Examples were exercises on order of magnitude estimation (e.g., how fast does your hair grow in metres per second and how many layers of atoms per second is that?), or interpreting graphs (given an oral account of a car journey, compose distance–time, velocity–time, and acceleration–time graphs to represent it), or planning investigations (observe different-sized marbles dropping into a tray of sand and make up a plan for investigating the formation of the craters). For many of these exercises, I often went into a seminar thinking that the problems that my colleagues and I had planned were too trivial. We invariably discovered that all our classes had found the problems challenging, and so we realised that skills that we assumed were so trivial that they would be picked up by informal osmosis were actually quite difficult for the beginner. They had to be taught (Black, Griffith, & Powell, 1974).

Concentrated Commitment

Most radical of all was the institution of what were called Group Studies in the final undergraduate year. The plan here had its origin in three considerations. One was the concept of concentrated study. Professor King at MIT had already described a course lasting a few weeks in which physics undergraduates had studied a single topic full-time. I and my colleagues had our own experiences of the rapid learning that could be attained if one were to study one topic rather than several at once; mine was a full-time one-week course in computer programming, where I went from knowing nothing to writing and running successfully a programme for analysis of my own research data.

A second consideration was that a weakness in investigative projects lay in the lack of serious study of the theoretical background on which the design, and the analysis of the results, had to be based. Unless this could be tackled, the final-year projects might not be any significant advance on those done in earlier years. So arose the idea of students working in seminar groups, each of about 20 students who would study together a particular physics topic. The plan was that these 20 would also work independently in four or five subgroups, each to carry out a different experimental investigation within the general area of the group's common topic. The work was to proceed by iteration between background talks prepared by staff and by students, and reports from each subgroup on the progress of their experiment. To deal with our whole cohort, we had to find staff willing to mount three such seminar groups, each with its set of four or five different experimental investigations.

A third consideration was that the work would be assessed as course work without formal written examination and that this assessment would play a significant part in the final decisions about the degree results. We were able to ensure that the work would be full-time in a period after all the students' formal written examinations had been completed, so that the students had no other study pressures.

The head of the department was intrigued, but also very concerned about both the risks of something so radical and the demands on staff time. He gave permission for one year only, with review at the end. It went famously. For the first time on record staff had difficulty getting students to leave the laboratory in the evening so that they could lock up. Within the groups, some students who had previously been no more than in the top quartile blossomed into being powerful leaders with initiative, whereas some of the other, previously "best," students emerged as good supporters of a group experiment rather than as leaders. Staff were hardworked because the students were often in a laboratory all day for several days on end and needed some attention. Assessment of the students took a great deal of planning, and was based on a variety of pieces of evidence: final project reports, quality of prepared talks for seminars, quality of talks on their experiments, and staff impressions of their relative contributions to each subgroup's experiment. We designed feedback forms on which the students wrote at great length. These were handed to the head of department. They were very strongly enthusiastic, and the experiment became a regular part of the degree course for many more years (Black, Dyson, & O'Connor, 1968).

In subsequent years, I met from time to time former students from the course. They usually mentioned Group Studies as a high point of their undergraduate learning. The outstanding memory for me was the realisation, evident in my earlier encounters with open-ended work but strongly to the fore in this innovation, that if students are given responsibility to tackle quite challenging tasks, they usually generate commitment and qualities of creativity and capacity to learn that come as a surprise. The learning style imposed in much of school and higher education fails either to evoke or develop this potential.

Communities of Learners: Providing HELP

On my return to university teaching after the excitement of the Nuffield A-level physics work, both my co-organiser, Jon Ogborn, and I thought that we could and should try to innovate also in university science teaching. It was clear that this should not be done through work on the curriculum: University professors would guard very jealously their control over what they thought best to teach. So we did not try to engage in content development but worked instead on teaching methods. We composed a proposal with junior staff in six university physics departments and asked the

Nuffield Foundation to fund a collaborative project between the six which would be called the Higher Education Learning Project (HELP).

The group decided to concentrate on four main areas of study. A first area was a research exercise based on interviews with undergraduate students. This will be discussed in chapter 6 on research. What is relevant here is that the parts of their courses that students judged to be positive learning experiences were laboratory projects, the preparation and writing of extended essays, and—to our great surprise—preparation for examinations. What these appeared to have in common were responsibility for one's work coupled with control over its organisation and timing, features that have been shown, in other research, to enhance learning.

In the other three areas, all six physics departments contributed ideas that they had developed in their own work, and then took some of the ideas of others and tried them out for themselves. We then tried to evaluate the work and to prepare written outlines to disseminate to others. Thus one area of work was focused on individual study. Some participant departments developed ambitious self-teaching exercises, stimulated by an American innovation known as the Keller plan in which entire lecture courses were replaced by monitored self-study. Wider adoption of the approach did not follow, perhaps because it called for radical changes in the organisation of undergraduate teaching.

The second of the three areas was small group teaching. Our Birmingham ideas for Skill Sessions were explored, a wider menu of ideas with examples developed, and outlines prepared to help replication by others. A similar set of outlines, called Tutorkit, was developed for the sort of small group tutorials with which I had struggled. In all cases the underlying idea was the same: to pass initiative to the students by means of tasks that were demanding yet feasible and from which all would learn useful lessons about learning needs. A study of verbatim transcripts of such tutorials carried out by Jon Ogborn brought out ways in which the fine grain of dialogue could promote or choke off useful discussion. In his collection of examples, one could see one's own mistakes and so learn to guide tutorials more fruitfully.

For the third area, attention was focused on laboratory teaching, where accounts of useful innovations were complemented by case studies of several teaching laboratories that the group visited as researchers, studying documents and interviewing academic staff, students, and the technical staff. This work alerted me to a new aspect. Each of the learning contexts that we were studying were distinctive social groups, with their own conventions, of behaviour, language, and relationships, that could promote or inhibit the quality of the learning. This perspective made clear that whilst we might usefully describe novel ways of working that had achieved success, mere reproduction of them as recipes would not guarantee success elsewhere. The case studies served to alert and sensitise other teachers to the conventions and language in which they themselves were immersed so that they could find their own paths to improvement.

The project's work led to publication of four books (HELP, 1977), which had a modest impact but are still used to this day. There was also a later influence: About 15 years later a group set up by the heads of university physics departments in the United Kingdom to review their courses concluded that they were attempting to cover too much material in the three-year degree courses. The proposed solution, subsequently implemented, was to change the normal course from three years to four, without increase in content, in order to allow more time for developing proper understanding. The teaching ideas and the research evidence in the HELP publications were quoted in this report, in part to show what could be done to enhance understanding if more time were available.

JOINT REFLECTIONS ABOUT TEACHING AND LEARNING

Much of what we have learned from our experience is general, in that it applies to most activities in teaching and learning. However, some of the lessons are specific, reminding us that each subject discipline has its own characteristics and problems. For science, some teachers and curriculum developers have focused so exclusively on presenting the subject in a pedagogically suitable manner that essential features of the discipline have atrophied or even vanished.

The link between actual practice of a discipline and its representation in education will always be problematic. But if the connections are too strained, the purpose of teaching the subject at all may become questionable. Thus, discovery learning may seem an attractive child-centered pedagogy, but it loses sight of the fact that the invention of some of the most productive science concepts was an act of rare genius. Similarly, the idea of "process-only" science takes the conceptual burden off the shoulders of teachers, which some might welcome. However, it so bowdlerizes the nature of scientific activity that it no longer seems worthy of a place in the curriculum.

Such deviations apart, there remain problems about pedagogy that are of specific importance to science and that are yet to be resolved. Outstanding among these is the implementation of "inquiry" in the United States or "investigation" in the United Kingdom as a key component of the learning of science (see chapter 1). Examples of excellence in this area are far from commonplace. Some teachers are adept at these approaches and create classrooms that are vibrant, both with energy and with science. However, activities of this type also can become routine and educationally vapid. It is necessary to exercise careful choice and guidance to determine which ideas are worth time in the curriculum. The visions that power such conceptions and that are proffered in the American national standards and the English national curriculum are certainly worthy, but they need far more patient investment in the support and evaluation of classroom work if they are ever to become reality.

Our Conclusions

More generally, our paths have taught us several lessons about learning that are now central to our vision. Like many other teachers, we often over-estimated the effectiveness of our efforts. We lacked the sensitivity to understand whether or not students were making sense of what we thought we were teaching. Because we often savored the educational diet we were offered, we did not fully grasp until we were well into our careers that many students may not have developed the same appetites. We came to realize that we, like all teachers, must seriously enter the student's world if we are to fathom what they know and how they might achieve the educational goals we desire. For that to happen, it is essential to listen to students, to draw them out, to have genuine conversations about their attempts to understand what we want to teach.

For such conversations to happen, it is necessary to shift the priority from an emphasis on delivery of instruction to one of designing and organizing settings where such talk is valued. In such surroundings, students begin to see the importance of their own roles in advancing their own education. In creating such environments, teachers must develop a clear concept of the nature of the learning aims that justify any activity, particularly if it is novel; if they lack such clarity, the work is likely to miss its target and lead to wasted opportunities. But that is not enough: The students also need to be active participants. In activities in which we helped to achieve such a shift of emphasis, or where we saw other teachers do it, we came to comprehend what many progressive educators had long asserted: Many students have unexpected educational potential that can flower in new learning environments but that remain undetected in conventional classroom settings.

None of these realizations are remarkable or new. However, they are more salient in current educational discourse than they were at the start of our careers, and they have been the stuff of endless debate, often sadly marked by stereotyping and demonizing of "progressives" or "traditionalists." Our own understanding of these matters has been enriched by opportunities to see many classrooms, talk with many teachers, and deliberate in many policymaking bodies. To the extent that our views are penetrating or subtle, they have evolved in such settings. And the most useful lessons we have learned have come from knowledgeable teachers rather than from treatises on pedagogy.

Experienced teachers have a wealth of craft knowledge that needs to be tapped in any enterprise to improve schools. It wouldn't be easy, but we might all start to do better if the potential of this source were to be acknowledged. Such a source does not have the tidy structure that has informed much of the research in education from which we might have learned, but did not. Such research might become more meaningful, and therefore more useful, when it can be so reconceptualized that it can better accommodate the complex, subtle, and deeply contextualized craft knowledge that informs the work of our best teachers.

5

Assessment and Evaluation

Evaluation and assessment have been central features throughout the professional career of each of us, with assessment of students being central for one, evaluation of educational programs for the other. As much as any aspect of education, evaluation and assessment are contested territories. They usually require the expression of educational aims in concrete, operational terms. But assessing a student's ability to state the law of gravitation is one thing. Gauging the student's skill in using the concept to compare the effect of gravitation at the surface of two different planets is another. And appreciating the depth and creativity of Newton's insight in relating the falling apple to the falling moon is quite another.

Assessments and evaluations are the bottom line in two senses. First, they make concrete what the curriculum actually is intended to accomplish. It is no surprise that this job is a tough one. It is easier to project a general goal than it is to specify just how that goal translates into actual work in classrooms. To avoid the challenge, however, is to risk commitment to aims that can be vague or even contradictory. Yet the move toward specificity runs a different risk: Highly explicit goals can narrow the curriculum undesirably. At an increasingly common extreme in both our countries, it can reduce the curriculum to those elements that are most easily assessed.

Second, assessment provides the main currency for public accountability. It is the bottom line in the sense that it is seen as the only procedure sufficiently solid and objective to justify investment. But it carries its own problems. It is a notoriously delicate and difficult task to fashion assessment techniques that simultaneously command the confidence of the public and also exert positive and helpful pressures on teachers and students. Few educational systems claim to bridge these two functions; in fact, one is often counterproductive to the other.

The symptoms of the pathology are well known: cramming, rote learning, high stakes on a single instrument, teaching to the test. Many teachers can be forgiven for seeing testing, and any associated measures implemented in the name of accountability, as oppressive, so that they keep it on the margins of their work for as long as possible. This disjuncture is serious, in itself and because it reflects and exacerbates a tension between the aspirations and values of teachers and the expectations and understanding of the rest of society.

For both of us, albeit in very different ways, our understanding of these issues and our appreciation of their importance have evolved over many years and through many experiences. The exploration of this aspect of our histories should serve to provide grounding for the views that we now share. Assessment is a central component of education. Yet, despite over a century of endeavor, public education has yet to achieve systems that can claim to resolve the inherent tensions in fully defensible ways.

MIKE'S STORIES

Evaluating Curriculum Programs: Defensive Reactions

With all the NSF-supported curriculum development activity that had been launched in the United States by the early 1960s, voices began to be heard about the need for evaluation. Publicity about these initiatives gradually increased, especially after the launching of Sputnik I in 1957. Lots of money was being spent to improve education. What were the results?

Two kinds of responses emerged from the evaluation and assessment communities, both with some similar features but also with an important difference. Simply put, assessment experts said, "Test the students to learn the worth of the program." In the United States, there was a strong history of paper-and-pencil testing of individuals that went at least as far back as the personnel classification examinations of World War I that determined whether a new soldier would be an infantryman, a mechanic, or a typist.

The other response was from the newer field of program evaluation. It, too, relied heavily on student testing, but it was coupled tightly with the objectives of the program under examination. This approach was pioneered by Ralph Tyler in the 1920s and 1930s (Tyler, 1949). A giant not only in the measurement and evaluation field but also in education and social sciences generally, Tyler later was social sciences dean at the University of Chicago and first director of the Center for Advanced Study in the Behavioral and Social Sciences at Stanford University.

"Tell us about the aims of your new curriculum, and we, the evaluators, will find out by testing the students how well you are meeting your own goals." The Tyler Rationale sounded logical. But by the 1960s it also had some added wrinkles. Not only was the curriculum developer to list the objectives of the program, they were to be stated in behavioral terms. What, specifically, were the students expected to *do* as evidence that they had learned? By means of the appropriate tests, it would then be possible to ascertain the degree to which curriculum objectives had been met, and thereby provide the data necessary to judge the success of the program.

I started to worry. Not unlike many people who develop something they believe to be original, I feared that neither of the approaches to evaluation then in use could adequately grasp what we were doing in the astronomy project. The tests for students being used to assess science achievement tended to stress the acquisition of discrete bits of factual information. The objectives-oriented evaluation procedure seemed atomized: The demand for identification of specific and detailed objectives often led to long lists of minor facts that seemed to obscure the more comprehensive picture. It ran the risk of riveting student attention on small bits of science content in ways that made interrelationships among them opaque.

We in the astronomy project cared much less that students know the order of the planets from the sun than that they have an understanding, for example, of how it was possible to build a scale model of the solar system without knowing any absolute distances. We cared less about the phases of the moons of Mars than that students understand the evidence that supported an Earth-centered view of the solar system over a heliocentric one. It did not seem to us that test makers had much experience assessing such outcomes, or even that they appreciated the elegant astronomical story line we thought we had developed.

A level of aesthetic appreciation, often wonder, is seldom far beneath the surface for people who know their subject well. Presumptuously, perhaps, we believed we were introducing students to profound, moving, and powerful ideas that would be ignored or trivialized by those who gauged program quality on the basis of readily discernible changes in student behavior.

We were concerned also about the limits on the curriculum that would be imposed by diligent and focused pursuit of stated objectives. Some of the most inspired and memorable teaching occurs unexpectedly. Unless teachers can be somewhat opportunistic, they might miss some of the most teachable moments. Every American teacher of eight-year-olds considers it important to teach children about sportsmanship. Few teachers of eight-year-olds plan a lesson on sportsmanship for 10:00 next Thursday afternoon. The best time for such instruction is when the class witnesses an unsportsmanlike act. So, too, with some ideas in science. If understanding the range of structural symmetries is an important biological idea, then it would be an unusual science teacher who did not digress during a field trip on some other subject to point out unanticipated examples of organisms displaying spherical or bilateral symmetry. Certainly no geology teacher who had planned a lesson on the effects of wind erosion would hesitate to drop it if an earth tremor had occurred in the community the night before.

Behavioral Goals

There was at least one further problem. In the application of the objectives model of evaluation, not only were the goals behavioral and therefore relatively concrete and unambiguous, they were always proximate. Progress toward them was to be assessed as learning took place. We believed, on the other hand, that many of our most significant goals were sometimes long-term and elusive. Take powerful and pervasive concepts such as equilibrium or randomness—or the idea of spherical symmetry mentioned in the preceding paragraph. Our view was to introduce the students to the idea, but often briefly because much of the power of the concept inheres in its ubiquitousness. Equilibrium and randomness are found in hundreds of contexts. They even transcend the distinct subject matter disciplines. We believed that some of these powerful ideas best grow slowly for the student. We even took the view that it was possible that early delineation and articulation of a very broad idea or theme like equilibrium might impede further development of it by providing a concreteness that could be limiting. Whether or not we were correct, this reason was one more that gave us pause about the desirability, for pedagogical purposes, of trying to pin down and encapsulate each of the major concepts primarily so they could be readily assessed.

We also viewed the new evaluation pressures with alarm because the procedures being advocated had at least a surface plausibility. Gauging results on the basis of goals seems reasonable and logical. It seemed to appeal to a general public that expected accountability. As a matter of fact, "management by objectives," a first cousin to the Tyler Rationale, was becoming a business tool among the most advanced corporations: Gauge how well an enterprise was performing its function by determining the match between its goals and its outcomes. Robert McNamara, head of the Ford Motor Company in the 1960s, was turning heads in the business world by applying the technique to one of America's largest corporations. When he became President Kennedy's secretary of defense, he brought the technique to the federal government. For good or ill, it proved a powerful tool in helping non-specialist elected officials exercise their authority over the experts in a given field. In deciding on directions and budget for the Department of Defense, he would ask the competing admirals and generals to specify the objectives in concrete terms for the military systems they wanted to build. What kind of firepower did they want to deliver, and under what circumstances? Could the navy do the job less expensively than the air force? How much would it cost the army? In short, how much bang for the buck could be obtained for the hard-pressed taxpayer?

Whether the outcomes were wise or not, the idea was taken up. McNamara thereby was able to exercise civilian control over a specialized military. The accomplishment so impressed Lyndon Johnson, who by then had succeeded Kennedy as president, that he decided to employ management by objectives throughout the federal government. Seminars were arranged wherein experts from the business world and the Department of Defense could instruct managers in all the federal departments on how to judge the success of their programs by determining the correspondence between performance and objectives. Civil servants in the (then) Department of Health, Education, and Welfare were among the most enthusiastic implementers of the plan. It was soon applied to some of the largest federal programs in education, including Head Start for preschool children and the compensatory education programs in school districts that served mostly low-income families.

In the light of our belief in the long-term nature of some of our most cherished curriculum objectives, and what we saw as their subtlety, we feared that the objectives-oriented evaluation tail would wag the curriculum dog. The curriculum would devolve to what could readily and quickly be assessed by the then-current examination procedures. Besides, we really did not know how we could subdivide the broad, long-term, and elusive objectives for which we strove into the kinds of assessment-sized bits that were demanded by the evaluators. The task was all the more daunting because the evaluators expected the curriculum developers to come up with the behavioral specification.

Criticizing Evaluation Models: Finding Allies

I began to write critically about the new evaluation expectations in curriculum, but only apologetically and tentatively, and as a person being subjected to them, not as an expert in the field (Atkin, 1963). To my relief if not my surprise, many of my fellow curriculum developers rallied around. To my surprise as well as my relief, some experts in evaluation raised similar questions. Michael Scriven, an internationally known figure in the field, wrote of "goal-free" evaluation, for example. It was insufficient, he said, to evaluate a program on the basis only of its declared objectives. What else was the program doing that was noteworthy and that a "consumer" might want to know?

Essentially the objectives model closely matches engineering procedures, and probably was drawn from that field. It is no accident that it flourished in the Ford Motor Company. Outline the specifications for a product, then gauge its success by how well it meets the specifications. But questions were being raised at the time about the engineering model itself. Is a product always considered successfully engineered if it meets its desired objectives? What about side effects? What about long term effects? A car can be designed and built to travel at speeds well over 100 miles per hour. The cost might also be relatively reasonable. But what if the car causes high levels of carnage on the highways? What if it consumes extravagant amounts of fuel? Side effects like these may not have seemed important when the automobile was designed, but public priorities change. Safety and the cost of fuel can come to be have social and political priority. One person's side effect becomes another's main effect.

So, too, in education. It may initially seem sufficient that a new program designed to teach reading actually does so, and even more quickly than another. But what if it turns out that students taught by the new method actually read less than similar children taught differently? Such a result can and has occurred. An apparent explanation is that the methods used in the experimental program are considered by the students to be aversive. They might learn the subject, even well by some criteria, but they also learn to dislike it. Science education is full of such examples. Students are sometimes taught chemistry through an onslaught of definitions, facts, and formulas. Even if they eventually earn high grades, some of them never again take a chemistry course. Shouldn't evaluators collect such information?

It turns out that these ideas were valued and nurtured at a unit called the Center for Instructional Research and Curriculum Evaluation (CIRCE) in the College of Education at the University of Illinois. This group was hospitable to the criticisms I was voicing. In fact, they were making many of their own. Robert Stake, a well-regarded psychometrician-turned-evaluator, was developing models of evaluation that were responsive to the clients who commissioned them and more faithful to curriculum goals. What sorts of information did a curriculum developer need to make the curriculum better? What kinds of evaluations were useful to the people who commissioned them? The evaluator might be critical of the program being evaluated, but some of the criticism, at least, would be on the wavelength of those with a stake in the outcome.

The Stake-Easley Project

With CIRCE's encouragement and support, I became involved in a large project that the University of Illinois undertook to find out what science was being taught in the United States, and how. Its origins lay in the fact that education activities within the National Science Foundation came under sharp congressional threat in the 1970s. The Tenth Amendment to the U.S. Constitution stipulates that all functions not specifically delegated to the federal government remain responsibilities of the individual states. Education is not mentioned in the Constitution. Some people felt the NSF had no business tampering with the curriculum.

Major figures at the NSF believed the entire foundation was under attack. It was decided to suspend curriculum improvement activities below university level immediately. However, the education group within the foundation, to sustain at least a bit of momentum for curriculum work, proposed that the NSF undertake a study of the state of science, mathematics, and social studies education in the United States. While the focus would be on existing practice, one purpose would be to find out the continuing influence of the NSF curriculum projects of the 1950s and 1960s. This kind of study by a unit of the federal government had ample precedent. The office of the U.S. Commissioner of Education had been collecting data about schools since the late 1800s.

The NSF decided to take a three-pronged approach to determining the state of education in science, mathematics, and social studies. One study would focus on what existing research and other published material had to say about the subject. The contract went to Ohio State University. One study would find out all that might be possible through survey techniques. What course preparation did teachers have in the subjects they were to teach? What instructional materials were used? How much time was spent teaching science (and mathematics and social studies) at different grade levels? How old were the teachers? How much experience did they have? The contract went to the Research Triangle Institute's Iris Weiss in North Carolina. The third was to develop case studies, descriptions in depth, of science teaching in selected schools around the country. The contract went to CIRCE at the University of Illinois. Bob Stake and Jack Easley were the co-directors.

I was dean of the College of Education at Illinois at the time. While my role in the new project was not large, I participated in many of the meetings that discussed sampling, case development, cross-case analysis, ethical issues, and much more. I met at length with all the case writers, each of whom spent about six weeks at one of the 13 sites chosen for the study. The sites were selected systematically on the basis of factors such as suburban/urban/rural, large and small, rich and poor, East/Midwest/South/West. A "site" was defined as a high school and its feeder elementary and middle schools. I also visited two of them. I was involved also in my role as dean, as it was one of the largest grants administered within the college.

The National Science Foundation released the results of the three studies simultaneously. They caused quite a splash, but I noted that the lion's share of press attention was given to the Illinois case studies. They showed primary reliance in science instruction on the textbook. The prevailing instructional mode was the whole-class recitation method. In elementary schools, almost all teachers digressed from a focus on math or science if the opportunity arose to teach about moral virtues like neatness or punctuality. There seemed to be little evidence in the schools that were visited of any of the curriculum improvement projects that the NSF had supported in the 1950s and 1960s. Some of the textbooks had bits of material drawn from these projects, but they were seldom introduced with the same intention of encouraging student inquiry that was so important to the developers. The fact that the case studies got most of the attention was unmistakable. My assumption was that the incidents highlighted in the cases, with real stories of classroom events, were more compelling to readers than survey results or summaries of research.

A Formative Evaluation

In 1995, the NSF was supporting a collaborative effort called the Leadership Institute for Elementary Science (LITES) to improve science teaching in Oakland's 60 elementary schools. It brought teachers from the school district into regular associations with faculty at nearby Mills College and staff from several museums and outdoor education centers in the neighborhood. The aim was to enrich the teachers' science knowledge and improve their teaching. The Mills professor who directed the project asked me to undertake a three-year evaluation of the project with the help of assistants from Stanford University, and I accepted.

The concept of *formative* evaluation, as contrasted with *summative*, was first articulated in the late 1960s (Tyler, Gagné, & Scriven, 1967). The evaluation work at Mills illustrates an effort not primarily to monitor or judge an educational program, but to improve it.

Mills is a small, distinguished, private women's liberal arts college. It was established in 1852 and enjoys an excellent national reputation. The project aimed to identify 20% of Oakland's elementary school teachers who, after a specially designed program at Mills and the museums, would take the lead in assisting the other 80% to teach "more and better" science. The program for the 20% mostly entailed special summer courses extending over three years at Mills in four science fields: physics, chemistry, biology, and earth sciences. Additional science content was taught at various museums and outdoor science education centers during the school year, usually on weekends. Additionally, there were Mills kit-based courses in

Guided Discovery (inspired by the Atkin-Karplus Learning Cycle, chapter 4) and Managing Change. The former was a course on methods of teaching science at the elementary school level. The latter was action–research oriented and designed to help the teacher leaders to figure out the best site-level approaches to improving science teaching within their individual schools. Teachers were compensated through the NSF grant for their involvement. Mills faculty received extra pay. The main association between Mills and the schools during the school year was the responsibility of three Oakland "teachers on special assignment" (TSAs), who also taught Guided Discovery during the summer.

My own interests lay primarily in studying the program itself to ascertain, for example, what was being taught to the teachers who came to the campus and why, how the teachers reacted, what the Mills staff expected of the teachers as a result of their participation in the program and how those expectations were conveyed, how services were being provided at school level by the TSAs, how the 20% changed science teaching in their own classrooms, the various ways in which the 20% worked with the 80%, and how the Oakland teachers and administrators might wish to continue project-related activities after NSF support was terminated. The members of the Stanford evaluation team would certainly spend lots of time in classrooms, but primarily to find out from teachers and children how the nature of science teaching might have changed since the advent of LITES, not precisely what the students learned as a result.

Handling Unpleasant News

All evaluation has the potential to be threatening, so I made it clear to the project director at the outset that I liked what I saw about the program. Indeed, I did not accept evaluation assignments for projects I did not admire. (Few evaluators hold this view. The stance is controversial.) Oakland is a school district with high percentages of low-income and non-white students. Teacher turnover is high. Neighboring institutions with special competency in science could be useful resources for a busy and often beleaguered cadre of teachers and administrators who were working with students who didn't seem to have the educational advantages of those in nearby and more affluent communities. The project staff at Mills was capable and energetic. Nevertheless, the Stanford evaluation group almost surely would encounter aspects of the program that were not working as well as they might; indeed, that possible outcome, along with suggestions for program improvement, was the purpose of our involvement. It would be the staff and director's choice whether or not to make program changes based on our analysis. The process, however, might be painful.

I urged the director to read a case study that several Stanford doctoral candidates and I had just completed of a major American curriculum project, the AAAS's Science for All Americans (Project 2061), for the OECD. We had found much to commend. We were generally admiring. But we also developed certain impressions about aspects of the initiative that the 2061 staff found questionable, even inaccurate. That circumstance led to extended discussions and considerable tension. We modified the report (for the better, in my view) as a result of probing more deeply into the perspectives of people at project headquarters. But there were still issues on which the Project 2061 staff disagreed sharply with the evaluation team, and that could not be resolved. In the end, we accorded a key figure from the 2061 group the opportunity to write a commentary on the Stanford evaluation. He took up the invitation and carefully laid out his objections to the study, primarily pointing out what he saw as initial bias on the part of the evaluators toward according teachers significant and early roles in curriculum development. Without editing it in any way, we incorporated his commentary into the published version of our case study immediately following our report (Raizen & Britton, 1997). He had the last word.

There were many elements of the project that were exemplary and unproblematic, of course. The TSAs were extraordinarily responsive to requests from teachers. The project was viewed within Oakland as one of the few initiated outside the system that could be depended upon to deliver what was promised. Teachers welcomed the chance to come to the Mills campus, where they were treated with a level of respect they did not always get from their administrators. Many of them relished the chance to work with peers in addressing new intellectual challenges in the Mills courses.

There were also problems. It wasn't clear that the school district had a clear commitment to the project. Science professors from Mills were expected to provide some services directly to teachers in their schools during the school year, but it seldom happened. Some of the science content most useful to the teachers was learned at the museums and outdoor education centers, yet these institutions were rarely highlighted in the program's publicity—and they weren't happy.

The Stanford-based evaluation group made frequent reports to the Mills staff about these developing perceptions of areas wherein the project might be falling short of its own expectations. In effect, we held up a mirror that reflected what we were seeing and the impressions we were developing. The questions we always asked at such meetings were, "Do you see what we see?" and "Do our inferences seem reasonable to you?" Sometimes we were corrected. Sometimes it was pointed out that what we had noticed was not imaginary, but reflected an isolated and unrepresentative event. More often than not, Mills staff found that our comments had a ring of truth, so they took action to make changes.

For another example, the TSAs, in their extraordinary responsiveness to requests from schools and teachers, seemed not to have developed their own priorities. In fact, they were running themselves ragged, we believed, to meet all the demands on their time. Should they have some set of guidelines to be used in responding to requests? Wouldn't targeted efforts be more productive? And wouldn't the added level of rationality in their professional lives produce greater satisfaction for them? The questions seemed sensible to them. They certainly felt harassed. They subsequently devoted considerable time and effort to developing a rubric for considering and prioritizing their work in the schools.

We saw examples like these as illustrative of how we wanted our formative evaluation to work. The evaluators helped to shape the conversations that project staff conducted in their deliberations about how their own work might become more effective. We participated in the subsequent conversations if our comments were desired—and they usually were.

Not all our observations were taken seriously or acted upon, of course. Governance and administration seemed to us rocky at several levels of the project. The Mills staff with by far the strongest connections with the schools and teachers were the TSAs and other nonprofessorial staff at Mills. In fact, the only full-time professionals in the project were in this group. Tensions with the professors and those officially responsible for the project sometimes were high. The full-timers believed that they had the deepest knowledge about the program, but that many of the key decisions about its directions, and about actions that they themselves would have to take, were made without their sufficient participation in the deliberations.

The project director wasn't always pleased with our analysis. Though she was unstinting in her public and private praise of what we had done to improve the program, she said that we tended to view the project from the perspective of the TSAs, which was probably true; they were the people we saw most often during our visits to Mills, schools, and classrooms. Clearly, formative evaluation can be as threatening as summative.

Student Assessment: Mike's Postscript About Teachers

In little of the evaluation work I conducted did we pay systematic attention to student test scores. Rather, our focus usually was on making the program better in the ways that the curriculum innovators desired. We saw little relationship between the tests that were administered, either those developed externally or those devised by the teacher, and the outcomes that were desired in the new program. Typically, the tests consisted of short-answer questions, usually a combination of multiple-choice questions and those eliciting only brief responses. At best, the test scores reflected a pale reflection of the understandings that were intended. The teachers usually didn't seem to pay much attention to them, either.

Nevertheless, even in the days of the astronomy project, some sort of student assessment was expected in new curriculum initiatives to satisfy the funders that the students were learning something. We knew little about measuring for deep conceptual understanding of the type for which we strove, however, so we never tried to develop our own exams based on the content we were trying to teach. Benjamin Bloom's *Taxonomy of Educational Objectives* had been written a few years earlier (Bloom et al., 1956), so we had a way of classifying questions based on a hierarchy of comprehension that he developed (recall, comprehension, application, evaluation, for example). However, none of our group were test makers and the taxonomy had been used little by the early 1960s, so we did not follow up.

Instead, we asked a person who had developed a commercially available short-answer *Test on Understanding Science* (TOUS), Leo Klopfer, to help us think through the kinds of questions we might give students to ascertain how much they understood about the nature of science. The astronomy project, we believed, offered special opportunities for students to learn about how science knowledge is generated and tested, the nature of scientific evidence, and how scientists attempt to refute and support theories. One of Klopfer's associates joined us for two summers to develop a version of TOUS that we could administer to students.

The results seemed to indicate that the students were learning something about what the TOUS-like test was measuring. They registered modest but significant gains when given before-and-after versions of the instrument. But we never used the test on a large scale, both because there seemed to be little interest in the outcomes we were measuring and because we ourselves weren't satisfied that knowledge about the nature of science as an enterprise was all that we intended to teach.

Student assessment seemed a side issue to me and to many other curriculum developers. Test scores without doubt carried weight with the public, but did not encourage innovations of the type that did not lead to higher test scores on the familiar examinations. The tests, in turn, were never intended to gauge the value of new approaches to the teaching of science. They were, in fact, an impediment to change. I didn't see how they could possibly help, even the best of them, because they did not incorporate the teacher's knowledge about the students' strengths and weaknesses.

It wasn't until 30 years later that extensive interest in what assessment can do to improve learning, not solely measure results, began to gain traction in the education community. Paul Black and his colleague Dylan

Wiliam, an assessment expert, reviewed hundreds of studies of assessment in the classroom, that is, the kinds of judgments teachers make about students and students make about each other and themselves (Black & Wiliam, 1998a). The analysis of the research pointed clearly to the fact that such assessment, when it is incorporated in the teacher's instructional repertoire—as by giving certain types of feedback to students about how their own work can improve in quality—has a positive influence on how much children learn. What interested me, in particular, about this line of research was that teacher judgment and behavior are central to the process. The teacher is uniquely positioned to gauge what students know and don't know. Information is available to them over the course of weeks and months that no written test, even one that extends over several hours, can uncover. The Black and Wiliam review accented the importance of placing the teacher at the center of the assessment process if educational programs are to be improved.

PAUL'S STORIES

Formative: A By-Product of Quality?

In my university teaching, the idea of formative assessment never crossed my mind, but given that formative assessment is an essential part of good teaching, as my teaching improved, my practice of formative assessment developed, albeit unconsciously. So I can analyse in retrospect.

In the attempts to enliven my lectures, described in chapter 4, the evaluation conducted by David Boud was both formative for me and helpful in providing formative feedback from the students through his ability to explore their responses. I came to see that I was in touch with students' learning in a direct way through their responses that I evoked in the lectures. In particular, I learnt that the aims and structure that were the framework for the learning were not clear to them. And I learnt that this framework had to be shared with students if they were to come to guide their own learning.

Such strategic lessons came to the fore in other evaluation studies. We set up in Birmingham a voluntary interfaculty evaluation group. The members organised themselves into pairs, with each committed to being an evaluator for the other's teaching. The group as a whole adopted a common approach. The evaluator first talked to the colleague about the context and purpose of the lecture course, then attended a short sequence of the lectures, then talked to small groups of students to explore their views of the course, particularly in relation to the lecturer's view. This would inform the development of a questionnaire to all of the students. Finally, the evaluator would report back on findings to the lecturer.

One striking example was the evaluation of a course in geography. The lecturer was worried because examination results of the students had been disappointing. The evaluator formed the hypothesis that they had misunderstood the aim of the course, and this was tested by presenting to the students a list of proposed examination questions. Half of these were about the methods and principles that the topics discussed in the lecture were merely meant to exemplify. The other half were about the particular examples that had been used, as if the aim was to teach these as content to be learnt. The students were asked to rank them, with those most likely to appear in the examination at the top. The responses shocked the lecturer, for the students had chosen the content test items as the most likely. They had brought to his class assumptions about the nature of learning, probably instilled by preparation for examinations at school (Black et al., 1976).

Disastrous chasms can exist between teacher and learner. Whilst feedback can be very helpful in the short term and with the fine grain, it is also essential in relation to the larger picture lest the chasms go undetected, leaving the students to make their learning journey without a map, or even with the map upside down.

However, summative testing soon came to dominate my attention. My formative interests were to reemerge many years later.

Summative Assessment: Can You Trust the Tests?

Having set and marked summative tests for several years, I was provoked into thinking about them by being "volunteered" by my university department to give a talk on assessment to a meeting of a professional association, the Institute of Physics. A library search opened up my thinking. One outcome of the library search was that I seized an opportunity to explore reliability. Our examination for physics undergraduates at the end of their first year consisted of a single three-hour paper. Since the result could determine whether or not a student could continue in the course, there was a case for arguing that three hours might be too short. So with faculty colleagues I arranged an experiment using two three-hour papers in place of one. Each paper had the same structure and types of question, covered the same courses, and was set and marked by the same lecturers. Thus the two were parallel, as if this year's paper and next year's paper were being taken together. They were taken within two days of each other by the same students, who had been fully informed about our intentions (Black, 1963).

Of the 100 candidates, 26 were deemed to have failed the first paper, and 26 were likewise deemed to have failed the second. However, only 13 had failed both: thus it seemed that half of those who failed on a typical paper might have passed if they had sat a parallel paper on another occasion. The differences were more than marginal. For 32 students their marks differed by more than 10% between the two. The short-term effect was a decision to set two three-hour papers in the future, to enhance reliability, but also, by employing a greater variety of types of question, to enhance validity. Ever since that experience I have been concerned about the ethics of determining people's life chances on short tests tackled in the artificial context of the examination hall. It has also puzzled me: Why do people who might directly suffer from the consequences trust such methods without asking for evidence available on the reliability of the result? If one were to ask, of any public high-stakes examination in the United Kingdom, for an estimate of the statistical probability that one could be wrongly graded on the result, no answer could be given, even though it would be a feasible (but not trivial) task to obtain such estimates. Measures that account for some, not all, threats to reliability are more commonly available in the United States. However, a study of the standardised tests used in California (Rogosa, 1999) has raised the same concern by showing that for tests that seem to have acceptable measures of reliability there are alarmingly high chances that a student will be misclassified, which could lead to a wrong placement in a slow track to the detriment of future educational progress.

A second outcome of the talk for which I was volunteered was an invitation to join a working party of the Institute of Physics, set up to study examinations in physics. My particular contribution was to collect evidence, including examination papers and grading schemes, about the methods by which students were being assessed at the end of their undergraduate courses to determine their class of degree. In the analysis of this evidence, we used four categories of aims of the testing (derived from Bloom's taxonomy): remembered knowledge, simple understanding, solving of problems, and analysis and synthesis. We then determined, for each of the degree assessment systems, what proportion of their final marks could be assigned to each of these categories. The results (Black, 1968) were disturbing, mainly because of the wide variety. When the balance between knowledge and the higher order categories varied, between universities, from 60/40 to 20/80, how could degrees from different institutions be comparable? Almost equally disturbing was that the mean, over nine degree courses, for the knowledge component was as high as 43%. Furthermore, no institution had evaluated its work in this way. When one of our group repeated this survey 10 years later, the overall picture had hardly changed. Validity was being taken no more seriously than reliability.

Summative Assessment: Making a Difference Through Testing

Because I had taken a serious interest in examinations, Birmingham University appointed me as one of its four representatives on the governing body of the Joint Matriculation Board, then one of the largest operators of public examinations in England. The leader of our quartet was a professor of electrical engineering, Jack Allanson, who was to become a leading figure in national debates about public examinations. He set up a task group to review policy in the testing of the sciences at the advanced secondary school level, drawing into its membership several who had both research and practical experience in the field. I learnt a great deal from their assessment expertise. We produced recommendations that led to radical changes in the Board's examinations. Traditional papers with only one style of questioning that rewarded mainly rote learning were replaced by a collection of diverse instruments. Multiple-choice tests were introduced, with an emphasis on items that tested understanding, and with enough questions to cover most parts of the syllabus. Also included were short problem questions, longer problems, questions testing understanding of a passage about an application of physics that the candidates had not met before, and teacher-based assessment of laboratory work.

Two years later I had a chance encounter with a professor of metallurgy. He remarked that I had obviously been changing things, for his daughter, just then taking the revised examinations, had told him that it was now quite different: Before, you could learn it mainly by heart; now you had to be able to think and understand. It came home to me that there were about 20,000 candidates every year whose learning would be affected in this way. It was most unlikely that my contributions to research in physics, which were no more than respectable, would ever have such a widespread influence.

Summative Assessment: A Tailor-Made Product

The development of the Nuffield Advanced Level physics course carried with it responsibility for a new examination scheme. The examination boards had agreed to support curriculum innovations by developing examinations to reflect and so reinforce their aims. At the same time, they would monitor the quality so that they could guarantee the equivalence of the standards to those of traditional examinations at the same level. Thus the curriculum developers became examiners, and were free to fashion the examination to reflect the aims of their course.

The outcome was an examination with six components. Four of these were written papers spread over two three-hour testing sessions made up of a multiple-choice test, a test with about nine short questions to examine basic understanding and the capacity to tackle routine problems, a text passage to test capacity to understand and use a new communication about physics, and a set of essay-type questions. In addition, the examiners set a practical examination composed of eight short laboratory exercises, set up and overseen in their own schools by the teachers, and marked externally. Finally, each student had to conduct an individual laboratory investigation extending over about 10 hours and marked by the student's own teacher (Black & Ogborn, 1977b).

This variety of instruments served to secure validity. For example, since learning in the future was an aim of the course, it had to be reflected in the test of capacity to understand a new communication about physics. There was also the attraction that the variety would mean that candidates who had particular strengths, for example, excellence with practical skills or a capacity to synthesise ideas and write a fluent essay, would all have a chance to show their strengths. More support was added when it turned out that the correlations between the scores of the same candidates on the different components were modest, which meant that, given reasonable reliability, each was testing a significantly different outcome from the others.

We did worry about one written paper in which pupils had to choose three questions from the six provided and write responses in the form of short essays demonstrating synthesis and reflection about some overall themes of the course. The results were discouraging. The diagnosis was that the demand was unreasonable. If we were serious about evoking and rewarding reflective and synthetic writing about fundamental themes, it would have to be produced in environments more conducive to such work than the timed internment in an examination hall. Eventually this paper was abandoned and replaced by teacher assessment of an essay produced over time in the normal learning environment (Morland, 1994).

Practical experience had already accumulated in the United Kingdom about the administrative and other practicalities involved in using work assessed by a candidate's teacher as part of a public examination. Several investigations had shown that acceptable reliability could be achieved if teachers were given some training and clear rules and procedures. Such findings are crucial for assessment policy, because those activities that need assessment over extended periods of normal classroom time will not be taken seriously if adequate reliability cannot be attained; both learning and the validity of the examination will then suffer.

Two misunderstandings have inhibited public understanding on this issue. One is revealed by the doubts expressed about the reliability of teacher-generated results, which, however reasonable, have never been matched by a comparable concern about the reliability of conventional examining. The other is the failure to grasp the point that whilst external and affordable tests can do a great deal to reflect and improve the quality of education, there are very important aspects of learning with which they cannot deal.

I have presented accounts of this Nuffield examination to many audiences overseas. The richness and variety come as a surprise, and envy is often expressed. But the reaction is that it cannot be replicated. It is too expensive, or the reliance placed on teachers' assessment cannot be acceptable, or the open-ended response evidence cannot meet certain canons of reliability. Such obstacles are serious enough, but should policymakers accept them, or work to overcome them?

Summative Assessment: Surveying the Nation

My experience with the British government contract on national surveys of science performance has already been described in chapter 1, where the focus was on deciding on the aims to be assessed. Of relevance in this section are the problems of the testing itself. We had to express each of our six categories of science performance in a suitable collection of questions, and then, through trials in which pupils' responses were explored, refine the scope and boundaries of each collection.

Pupils' responses were often surprising in ways that cast doubt on the validity of a question, and even on the concept that underlay the specification of the category. The need to rethink the concept of "scientific observation," discussed in chapter 1, was one such case. Such feedback from pupils was used to refine the assessment scheme: We were operating at a level of sophistication that I had not previously met in conventional examining (Black, 1990).

We encountered further problems when a visiting academic interviewed pupils after they had tackled our questions. He found that when children were asked to explain their answers, they would often produce reasons that showed that their written responses did not reflect their understanding. For example, on multiple-choice items many who had selected a correct response would justify that selection using faulty reasoning. On open response questions, pupils were often so misinterpreting the intention that lay behind the wording that they failed to do themselves justice. It was all too easy to elicit an unfair picture of a pupil's achievement.

A related problem was that according to the type of question or the question context employed, one could produce very different measures for the performance of any one pupil in relation to the assessment aim. For example, a question about the design of an experiment might either give a list of the apparatus available or a photograph of the same apparatus: the mean scores on the latter were significantly higher than on the former.

In tackling these variabilities, we had to decide how far it was legitimate to narrow the definition of the domain of questions in order to reduce them. Then we had to determine how extensive a sample of questions was needed to achieve, by averaging over the remaining variations in the responses, an adequately accurate measure of the average performance for that domain.

The outcome was that for those domains tested by written tests, it turned out that to cover all the domains we needed samples that would take all 30 hours of testing. We were able to do this by dividing the questions into 30 separate one-hour tests and giving the different tests to different but carefully matched subsamples of the pupils, so that no pupil had to spend more than one hour—a constraint imposed to secure participation by schools. For "pupil investigation," for which we used one-on-one assessment of laboratory performance of empirical investigations, generalisation over the category of performance proved to be impossible. The time needed for external testing of a sample of questions large enough to ensure adequate accuracy was impractically long.

"Adequate accuracy" was in itself a concept that called for exploration. One criterion was that no one source of error, be it in administration, or in marking, or in domain sampling, or in the pupil sample, should dominate, for if it did so then the design could probably be improved by redirecting the available resources to strengthen the weakest link. A second criterion was that the results should be sufficiently accurate to enable exploration of those features which were specified in the government's aims for the project. Two government aims were salient. One was to identify areas, perhaps causes, of underachievement. Given accuracies within a few percent in each of our measures, it was easy to show regional and gender differences, and differences related to rural, outer suburb, or inner-city school locations. The latter were large, but this was a well-known effect and we could not explore it in detail because the teacher unions would not countenance the collection through schools of data on parental employment, income, or education. The second aim was to detect changes over time: With monitoring every five years over 20 or so years something might have been achieved, but we were required to test every year for five successive years and no significant change could be seen. At a very early stage I had questioned the logic of testing every year: No clear answer was forthcoming.

The programme of annual testing was abandoned in 1984, and our teams then worked on relevant research with a view to a restart for 1989 as part of a new five-year cycle. The onset in 1988 of national curriculum and assessment overtook these plans, and the monitoring surveys were abandoned. The government showed no interest in preserving the archives of questions or using the experience and data gained in the surveys. I came to regret that we spent too much time on reports for government and too little on publishing our work in the international literature.

This survey experience showed how the task of obtaining a full and reliable picture of school performance in any subject might best be tackled. Our scheme, using 30 separate one-hour tests taken by different samples, was accepted technically as an optimum design for the purpose. However, the British investment in this area has come to nought in the face of the political imperative to give all pupils the same test so that rankings of school performance could be published. Here, by stark contrast with the 30 hours, is a single two-hour test for all, which is far more expensive than a survey and yet must be a poor indicator for any purpose: There is no measure of what must be poor reliability, and it is seriously deficient in validity.

Formative into Policy: Feet to the Fire

In July 1987, I faced an interview with three senior officers of the ministry of education. I was overawed, for big changes in national education policy were afoot and I was being appraised for a part in the play. A national curriculum was to be framed, and I presumed that I might be on the group to advise on the science component of that curriculum. However, the discussion ranged more widely and I was enticed into talking about my experience and ideas in assessment and testing. Whilst I saw merit in the idea of a national curriculum, the accompanying talk of national testing worried me, and I gave my views on the dangers, and my speculations about the framework within which such dangers might at least be reduced.

The outcome, which came a few days later, was an invitation to chair the group to advise the minister on the new policy for national assessment and testing. I was both astonished and frightened, and considered refusal for this could be a poisoned chalice. Yet on the other side there urged the angel of moral responsibility. I had an opportunity to help make the best of the inevitable. As I engaged with the prospect, the vagueness of the brief and the influence I was given over the membership of the group made it seem possible that something useful could be achieved. A splendid group was convened and battled to produce, between mid-September and Christmas, a report that could form a basis for the implementation of the minister's new powers to establish national assessment.

The Task Group on Assessment and Testing, which came to be known as TGAT, achieved a more constructive consensus than one could have hoped for. Ideas were contested, and fears and dangers faced. The combined effects of the pressures, of time and of the heavy responsibility entailed, served to force us to move very quickly into a radical interrogation of underlying principles. The outcome was a set of recommendations for national assessment and testing based on four principles. One was that test results should reflect and report on each of the main learning criteria to be set out in the national curriculum. A second was that these criteria should be specified in a single sequence to chart the progression in learning of each pupil over the age range from 5 to 16. Thus the assessment results would record at each age the criterion level a pupil had achieved. The third was an assertion of the primacy of the formative function; the system was to be structured to support teachers' formative practices so that they would be helped to promote pupils' learning in the light of frequent feedback. The fourth, which followed in part from the third, was that the summative results of national testing should be determined by a combination of teachers' own assessments and the results of external tests (Department of Education and Science, 1988).

The principle that the support of learning is one of the purposes of assessment did feature in the original brief from the minister, but TGAT made it the centrepiece of a comprehensive framework for the new assessment and testing policy. This emphasis was one of several features of the TGAT report that caused surprise when it was published in January 1988. A nervous teaching profession came to welcome it. Many of the press were baffled, finding it acceptable but wondering whether or not we had pulled off a confidence trick. Prime Minister Margaret Thatcher was uneasy, as she later wrote in her memoirs, that anything welcomed by the teacher unions, the *Times Educational Supplement*, and the BBC couldn't be right (Thatcher, 1993).

The outcome was tragic. The first considered statement by the education minister accepted almost all of the proposals, including thereby a commitment to the primacy of formative assessment. Within a year he had been replaced. The statutory body that had been set up to implement the assessment policy worked almost exclusively on setting up summative testing. In its first five years, this body had formative assessment before it as a specific agenda item on only two occasions. It is hard to find a reason for this neglect. Cynically one can wonder whether the acceptance was purely cosmetic, made only to buttress professional acceptability. Or perhaps it seemed less urgent and tangible an issue than the establishment of controversial national tests, a task that ran into such problems that it absorbed all the available bureaucratic energy. Or again, it may have been assumed—wrongly—that the recommendations about formative assessment were merely a confirmation of existing practice, so that no new action was necessary.

A root cause for this outcome was that the need for national assessment was seen by government in very simple terms. Schooling had run out of control: Romantic child-centred views of learning had weakened the system. The cure was to specify what was to be taught and to use tests to put pressure on schools to make sure that they taught it. Those who might question this simple model were part of the problem that it was designed to cure. Right-wing critics argued that the minister had given people like me too big a say, and that whilst this might have been tactically wise in order to overcome initial opposition, once the legislation had gone through the TGAT indulgence in academic theory could be ignored. In such a situation, TGAT's scheme was a lost cause. The government's impetus could have been resisted if one had a power base, or if one could mount a strong body of public opinion in opposition. No power base existed, the teacher unions had been weakened through defeats in failed strikes, and public opinion on testing was as ill informed as the government's own.

In retrospect it seems clear that the TGAT argument for formative assessment lacked both the substance and the incisiveness that it might have conveyed had there been time to study and reflect upon what was been proposed. About 10 years after TGAT, in the course of a literature search, I came across a paper in a journal called *Exceptional Children*, of which I had never before heard, let alone read. It reviewed 21 published articles containing data on 96 experimental effects that produced firm quantitative evidence that attention to improving formative assessment would raise standards significantly, which meant that attention to formative assessment could contribute to the principal aim of government policy.

The TGAT report contained no reference to any evidence that formative assessment could be so productive. The irony is that it could have done so because this article had been published in 1986. The search that unearthed this paper had its remote origins in the TGAT report, for after that experience I was determined to do further work on formative assessment. I shall describe this further work in chapters 6 and 7.

Summative Assessment: Testing Takes Control

Formative assessment was only one item, albeit with high priority, within the TGAT group's broad mandate of policy for national testing. The government priority was to have blanket national tests at ages 7, 11, 14 and 16, seen as a necessary part of the imposition of a national curriculum.

Most members of the TGAT group had long experience of both survey assessment and of the public examinations set at 16 and 18. They could not share the naïve public confidence in short external tests and anticipated that such tests would have negative feedback on learning. The proposals tried to alleviate these problems in several ways. A central feature was that the external test results should be combined with teachers' own assessments to produce the final results through processes of peer review in local groups using methods already developed for teacher-assessed components of public examinations. The government ruled that a local group system was impractical. They then fatally devalued teachers' assessments, first by ruling that their results should be published alongside those of external tests and not combined, and then by ruling that teachers should decide their assessments after the test results were available.

The concern about the invalidity and unreliability of short external tests was most strongly felt in relation to the proposed testing of the youngest pupils, who were the most likely to have problems with language and with understanding the purpose of the exercise. So rather longer assessment tasks were proposed in which pupils would work at a small project, rather like the good teaching exercises that the best primary teachers already used. These would be structured so that evidence of pupils' capability in various curriculum components could be gathered during their work. This proposal was taken up, contractors appointed, and trials conducted of their product. Reactions were mixed, but the tasks produced a heavy workload for primary teachers, not least because the practice of assessment amongst many of them was very weak. They could neither engage with the purposes of the tests nor see the reasons for the effort involved. Many complained, and the media made much of their complaints. In so doing they played into the hands of those who were suspicious of the complex proposals of TGAT and believed that its members were actually trying to undermine the national test proposals. A new education minister, Kenneth Clarke, quickly dismissed the exercises as "complicated nonsense," and written short external test papers took over.

Perhaps one fault in the TGAT report was that we failed to emphasise that any attempt to implement radically new assessment procedures is bound to fail if it is imposed without allowing teachers time to understand, and to influence, the changes. However, it would always have been hard to resist the simple attraction of a short test paper that yields lists of numbers so that all can see, without complex explanations, who is or is not doing a good job, and whether or not one's children are making good progress. Numbers particularly have a seductive power that can overcome the doubts that they might be at best inaccurate, at worst meaningless. If even the teaching profession itself is not well educated to understand these and related assessment and testing issues, there is little prospect that the general public will ever be dissatisfied with national testing.

Summative Assessment: Another Country

After the several years of the slow and steady unstitching of the TGAT principles, I made a protest speech at the annual meeting of the British Association for the Advancement of Science, which attracted some attention in the press. Britain's curriculum and assessment revolution attracted international attention, so I was invited in 1994 to lecture at the annual conference of the American Educational Research Association (AERA). This led to a publication in an AERA journal (Black, 1994) and an invitation to join a Board of Testing and Assessment (BOTA) that had been set up by the National Academy of Sciences.

Here I entered a different world. The range and high level of expertise around the committee table was impressive and, for me, rewarding. The dominance in the United States of standardised, mainly multiple-choice testing for all "high-stakes" purposes had fostered the development of very sophisticated expertise in the science of psychometrics, besides which some of the United Kingdom's procedures for public examinations seemed amateur. Yet this was also a fatally weak tradition. I had already had occasion to draw upon writings by leaders in psychology and in education in the United States who were warning of the very negative effects on learning exerted by testing pressures. The seriousness of these effects was becoming more obvious as theories and supporting evidence about the conditions for effective learning made progress.

So the United States was rich in programmes to develop new styles of assessment. The associated themes included "performance assessment," "authentic assessment," "portfolio assessment," and "curriculum-based assessment." But there seemed to me to be a weakness in overall strategy. From many of the published accounts it was difficult to see whether the innovation was aimed at improving formative assessment or summative assessment, or both. As they tried to provide, for example, new means to satisfy statewide testing that had the main purpose of accountability to the public, the new methods were subject to the requirements for reliability that were already expected of the standardised tests that they were meant to replace or supplement. Often they could not meet these expectations. It would have helped if their developers had studied the lessons about means to establish inter-teacher reliability, which could have been drawn from experience in Britain and in some of the Australian states.

More fundamentally, the whole rationale for the innovations lay in concern about the validity of standardised tests. Their reliability was not in question (although, as I have pointed out above, it ought to have been). To demand that more valid methods cannot be entertained until they achieve the reliability of less valid methods is to prejudge the argument about what would constitute an optimum system—the possibility of an inevitable trade-off between reliability and validity received too little attention.

In the work of BOTA, the discussions were constrained by the traditions of standardised testing, and the pressures and opportunities coming from various federal and national bodies were very often focused in terms of this taken-for-granted tradition. So it was hard to give salience to a concern for learning. However, this concern did eventually become a top priority and led to the setting up of a subgroup to study how the foundations of assessment should be rebuilt in terms of current theories of how people learn. The outcome of this work was a book that might encourage a positive shift in the terms of debate on testing (Pellegrino et al., 2001).

Every country is trapped in its own traditions and therefore in the practices and priorities that are taken for granted. Both the United Kingdom and the United States are no exceptions to this rule. International comparative studies have a great deal to offer in this respect. For example, how did it come about that the United States relies so heavily on multiple-choice testing; why is it that universities in eastern Europe have long believed that you can only select entrants on the basis of oral tests, as understanding can only be assessed through personal dialogue; and how is it that the Australian state of Queensland abandoned external tests in 1982 and relies on teacher assessments for all purposes? (See chapter 9 in Black, 1998). Given the intriguing nature of such questions, it seems a pity that the arena of international studies of science education has been taken over by international studies of pupil performance, based as these must be on short tests limited to the least common denominator of each country's aims and practices. This is not to deny the value of such studies, but to question yet again the seduction of numerical data. Each country can learn far more from others than merely their place in the league table.

JOINT REFLECTIONS ABOUT
ASSESSMENT AND EVALUATION

As we noted in the introduction, assessment and evaluation are central elements in the relationship between schools and the public. It is not surprising that misunderstandings and controversies about education cluster around these functions, for the terms and criteria by which they are conducted become the language for communication between the different stakeholders. Nor is it surprising that the misunderstandings are intertwined with conflicts about educational aims and values.

If there is one issue that recurs throughout our two accounts, it is that of validity. Do the tests actually measure what we value as outcomes of education? Indeed, can they ever do so without radical—and expensive—changes in their structure and orientation? Does an evaluation that shows impressive test score gains carry any guarantee that the students are better served by their teachers and their schools? Or do we need much more rounded and comprehensive pictures of what is happening in the classroom life of the students to make defensible judgments about the quality of our schools?

One reason why such questions are usually given far less attention than they deserve is the seductive power in our society of numerical measures. The comfort that they provide is usually illusory, however. When it comes to determining a student's life chances, like being chosen by a particular university (or going to university at all), the measures are far more prone to error than the public realizes. This alone should be a matter for serious concern, even if the measures really were a sound basis for making inferences about students' potential. But they demonstrably are not.

One feature of society's seduction with numbers is that it is hard for people to understand that the main errors do not arise from incompetence but are inherent limitations of any attempt to reduce the judgments of human beings to a few numbers. The figures take on a life of their own, with few people seeming to care about what they actually represent. Furthermore, in the current rhetoric of "standards" the numbers are trammeled in fatal confusions about norms of performance and criteria for deciding on a specific number. Thus, if a certain score demands higher performance, the standards will have gone up. But the result is that the number of students achieving that score will have gone down, so standards will have declined. It is uncomfortable for those in the policy field to face such issues. Indeed, Paul has met instances when senior figures in or close to government have said that to tease out and publish error data for public examinations should not be done because it would undermine public confidence.

Our Conclusions

Given this, it is hard to see how the radical changes in approach to the whole gamut of issues entailed in public accountability, evaluation of programs and of schools, and assessment of individual students could be tackled. What is needed is to replace simple unitary measures by a more faithful, and therefore complex, collection of qualitative and quantitative information. Of course, this would make the whole process more expensive, and make it far more difficult to make quick judgments when decisions have to be made about the futures of individuals and of institutions. There is inconsistency here. It would be rare to find a business or a government department that appraised its staff's progress and promotion prospects by setting aside all they knew about them, and using instead a single grade determined by a test delivered by an outside agency. Those involved outside education in procedures of this sort know well that the decision making that is required is rarely simple, and entails judgment among diverse criteria that can only be value judgments relevant to particular contexts.

What is at issue, however, is more than a set of problems only at the interface between education and society. Assessment, seen as feedback between teachers and learners, is central to the business of learning. The explicit recognition of this principle is now spurring many activities for school improvement, including our own current collaborative work involving teams at both Stanford and King's. Yet one obstacle to its further development is the pressure exerted by high-stakes tests. Under such pressure, teachers all too easily regress to the narrow drill and practice that they judge to be the best way to earn the approval that these tests promise to yield. Tests that were more sensitive to the task of exploring students' understanding would help to reduce such discordance, but externally designed tests can never meet all the requirements of valid assessment. Far more is needed, specifically ways to communicate the teacher's own knowledge of her students. She works with them day after day, month after month. She has information available to no one else.

Relying more on teachers' judgments in communicating to parents and the public would enhance the professional status of teachers. But that is a bonus. Validity of the assessment is the driving necessity. To be sure, such a development faces formidable obstacles. Fairness, validity, and reliability could only be ensured after patient development and training programs. Even so, teachers would have difficult problems in both helping their students and at the same time making, and subsequently interpreting, records of their work for the purpose of making judgments about quality. Through such development, however, teachers would come to share in ownership of any public testing scheme, rather than being victims of off-the-shelf tests. But more inclusive assessment should not stop there. Students also should be involved, and should share that ownership. As they become active agents in evaluating as well as pursuing their own learning, they learn about the nature of high standards and gain a greater understanding of the means for achieving them.

As academics acting from time to time as advisors to policymakers, we, like many of our colleagues, have encountered daunting dilemmas. To propose ideal solutions requiring several years to implement is to risk having one's ideas summarily rejected. To temper proposals to the prevailing political currents is to risk compromising one's scholarly expertise in support of the insupportable. The TGAT group was caught in such a dilemma.

At the same time, the bureaucrats are also caught in between, trying to select and influence the expert advisors so that they talk acceptable language, and to moderate the politicians so that they produce policies that might actually work. On the fringes, the media and the pressure groups, often in unholy alliance, are likely to seize on and exaggerate disagreements. Meanwhile, teachers, who all too often are given a voice only late in the day, will be confused, perhaps lost in the policy debate.

6

Educational Research and Educational Practice

How has educational research influenced science education? How is such research changing? We gradually are recognizing that if research is to connect with actual educational practice and influence it, it may have to encompass broader views of what counts as scholarly inquiry. For almost all of the 20th century, the goal of education research was to strive for broad principles with both explanatory and predictive power. The models for achieving the goal were drawn from the sciences: controlled experiments, random sampling, hypothesis testing, high-order generalizability. The results of such work, however, often seemed to have little impact on classroom practice. As a result, there is considerable methodological ferment in the education research community these days (as there is in the social and behavioral sciences communities generally). We know now that educational research is likely to be messier than most people might wish if it is to be taken seriously by those who presumably are its major audience: teachers, school administrators, policymakers, and the general public.

A few years ago, an evening session at the annual conference of the American Educational Research Association was devoted to a debate between two eminent figures in education research, Elliot Eisner, a former president of the association, and Howard Gardner, a Harvard psychologist. The proposition was that a piece of fiction, a novel centered on an educational context, could be a viable doctoral thesis in education. That such a topic could command a slot in the program would probably have been unthinkable two decades ago, yet on this occasion it filled the meeting room with over 300 of the research fraternity keen to both listen and take part in the discussion that followed.

Is this what "messier" might come to? Coming as we both did from the orbit of research and application of science, and then almost stumbling through curriculum development into the world of educational research, we struggled with two fundamental problems. One was that of the puzzled newcomer. What should we do that might count as research in education? The other was that of the practitioners with whom we had worked. Why was it that research in education seemed to have had so little impact, and in particular had not helped us in our earlier work in schools and universities? This chapter is the story of how we came, if not to answer such questions, at least to understand why the issues are so difficult.

MIKE'S STORIES

Getting Socialized at the University

I did not become concerned about a possibly serious disjuncture between education research and education practice until I had been a member of a university faculty for about five years. Coming from seven years of teaching in secondary and elementary schools, and despite my recently acquired doctorate in education, I was not deeply socialized into the world of the educational researcher. More to the point, I hadn't reflected much on the relationships between research in education, typically conducted at universities, and what teachers do in their classrooms. Unlike most of my new colleagues at the University of Illinois, whose background was in fields such as economics, sociology, psychology, philosophy, and history—and who had never taught in elementary or secondary schools—my professional identity and commitments were those of a science teacher. Thus I believed that educational research and scholarship was often interesting and occasionally produced something of value for schools, but it was hard to see that much of it could be consequential in the day-to-day life of a teacher.

This naïveté about education research seemed no great handicap at the time. As a professor and therefore advisor now to doctoral students, my role in the research process centered on the methods by which dissertation research was conducted and whether or not the student's conclusions followed from the evidence. Issues surrounding the contribution of the research to the education enterprise, in the sense of effecting improvement in schools, often were examined in a short introductory section of the dissertation and in an "implications" section at the end, but these matters were usually secondary. There was a ritual nod to the principle that a piece of research reaches beyond its own boundaries and is nested in a line of work with a past and a future, but those connections to a broader world were more often to other research on a similar topic than to educational practice.

Behavioral Science Theory and Educational Practice: Growing Doubts About the Connections

My early career at a research-oriented university, then, was centered primarily on my instructional responsibilities in teacher education and on curriculum development activities. Both fields were only beginning to be touched by perspectives from academia. Neither, in any deep sense, could be considered a well-understood or systematic scholarly enterprise at the time.

My view of the benign influence of educational research on practice changed when I became familiar with Robert Gagné's work *Science, A Process Approach* (SAPA), an NSF-supported project of the early 1960s (Gagné, 1966). Gagné was the project's guiding theoretician and researcher. He was an esteemed task-analytic psychologist who had developed his approach to curriculum development in the U.S. Army Air Force during World War II. Faced with the challenge of training thousands of technicians, Gagné and his colleagues had approached their assignment by analyzing a technical task for its subsidiary components, then developing instructional modules for teaching the requisite skills. If the job was to train radar operators, Gagné's group began by studying accomplished radar operators. To make sense of what they saw on the radar display, the operators had to be able to tune various dials to the necessary levels of precision. They had to know when and how to change distance scales. They had to discriminate among different images, and much more. Analyzing the complex tasks to identify all the necessary, subsidiary skills in such a fashion, the developers of the training programs learned that hundreds of specific and different operations are required.

Once the skills were identified, the course designers devised instructional sequences that taught the necessary prerequisite skills for the more complicated task, in sort of a skill pyramid with mastery of the entire operation at the top. Thousands of technicians were trained successfully and quickly for the military in such a manner during the course of the war. I was one of them. On entering military service at the age of 18, I was sent immediately to a program in the navy for the training of electronic technicians by the same methods devised and employed by Gagné and his colleagues in the Air Force. By the time I completed the one-year program, I was expected to repair any piece of electronic equipment in the navy, and could.

Applying Task Analysis in Schools

Was this to be the model for research on improving education in schools? It certainly was this approach, precisely, that was applied 20 years later to

SAPA. Gagné and his colleagues started with the conviction that the *processes* of science were to be the central elements of the course designed for grades kindergarten through six. (SAPA had an echo in the United Kingdom in a project called *Science 5 to 13*.) They started, as they had with the radar operators, by identifying accomplished scientists. They asked them about what they did and particularly about the processes they employed in doing their work. The scientists said, among other things, that they identified problems, and they observed, and they measured, and they sometimes formulated hypotheses, and they tested the hypotheses, and came to conclusions, and they applied the conclusions. The psychologists and instructional designers then took these statements of skills and developed instructional sequences for which the organizing principles consisted of the science processes that had been identified, topics such as observation, measurement, and hypothesis formation. (Scholars in fields like philosophy, history, and sociology of science, who often take a more nuanced view of the scientific enterprise, were not consulted.)

Thus the fact that one uses several senses in making observations was taught by having children pop corn. Knowledge of scientific principles illustrated by popping corn was not the objective of the lesson, however. The assumption was made that this activity helps the child to recognize the usefulness and limitations of sense experience; she or he can then more fruitfully observe the motion of a rolling ball or the growth of a mold garden.

The SAPA group assumed that science is sort of a commonsensical activity and that the appropriate "skills" are the *primary* factors in doing productive work. There was no explicit recognition of the powerful role of the conceptual frames of reference within which scientists and children operate and to which they are firmly bound, a perspective to which Karplus and I were deeply committed. I viewed SAPA as undesirably and misleadingly reductionist, missing a key element of science as an organizing principle: the subject matter itself (Atkin, 1966).

Confronting Academic Values

The viewpoint that emerged for me at this time marked the beginning of what came to be a major preoccupation in the years that followed. I started to confront academic research traditions directly in terms of the values they embodied, and specifically their connection to the world of classroom teachers. My incipient concerns intensified about the limited and sometimes misleading quality of many theoretical positions drawn from behavioral and social science and applied to education, such as task-analytic psychology. I began to raise questions publicly about the relationships between research and education—particularly research conducted on a presumed scientific model (Atkin, 1968).

Looking at the work of my colleagues in social and behavioral sciences, it began to dawn on me that teachers and other practical people can be studied and analyzed from any number of disciplinary perspectives. The research was often interesting. But any one discipline alone is but a monochromatic view of a multicolored classroom picture. Many sociologists study peer relationships and status differences in educational settings. Many anthropologists examine the role of an educational system in transmitting cultural values. Many psychologists conduct research on how children learn. Many linguists investigate the role of discourse in developing understanding and shared meaning. Often the research is rigorous. The findings are subjected to critical analysis. The investigators modify their approaches and conclusions in communities of their peers.

Problems arise, as I began to see them, when attempts are made to take the results from any one of these disciplinary perspectives and apply them to worlds of educational practice. The theories are anthropological, psychological, and linguistic. They are not educational. That is, they open a window onto but do not encompass all that a teacher must consider when working with a classroom full of children. Even the sum of research results from different disciplines can fail to address critical factors. What about the priorities of the teacher? What is she trying to maximize at any given time? What special knowledge does she have about the students with whom she works? These are just a few of the factors involved in a teacher's taking action about the classroom dilemmas they face. Even if a researcher tries to encompass all these considerations into the research focus, it is unlikely that a teacher faced with the necessity of taking action—even a seemingly mundane one, such as calling on one child rather than another—conducts an inventory of the principles that might apply before making a decision. There is a thought-*in*-action quality in the work of practical people that simply doesn't yield to conventional canons of behavioral and social science research.

Local Knowledge and Practical Theories

These last observations were tentative and undeveloped when I reacted negatively to SAPA's virtually content-free curriculum. But I came eventually to believe that local knowledge is almost everything in intelligent practice. General principles drawn from the education research literature are often both irrelevantly abstract and unworkably narrow.

But how does one then conduct research that has implications for teachers' practices? Is some sort of synthesis possible between the abstract generalization and concrete knowledge, between the timeless principle and the timely action? Teachers must be concerned with what is prudent in a given setting, what is obligatory, and what is moral. How can research be constructive and still apply to situations that are inevitably highly contextualized?

Professors, who work in universities and who receive the lion's share of support for education research, certainly live in a different world than teachers. This much I knew from personal experience. For one thing, teachers make dozens of decisions every hour that they work with a group of students—and they work with their students four to five hours every day. Some of the choices are excruciating. Do I call on Harry or Marian, both of whom have raised their hands in response to my question? Based on past experience, Marian probably will provide a helpful response and move the class along to the next point. Harry, on the other hand, is likely to go off on some interesting but tangential point. Harry, though, hasn't volunteered a comment in class for two weeks. This kind of choice, and dozens of others, confronts every teacher every day. To respond well is often crucial for individual students, for the kind of classroom atmosphere the teacher wishes to create, and for the curriculum concepts the teacher wants to teach.

Professors, in their roles as researchers, face different challenges. They are expected to generate new knowledge. Motivated by advances in science, many of those who aspire to understand and improve the human condition see themselves as social and behavioral *scientists*. In the process, they often develop stronger collegial relationships with researchers in fields such as psychology, sociology, linguistics, and economics than they do with teachers in schools. In the most distinguished research-oriented schools of education, there is usually pride associated with attracting outstanding scholars from fields such as psychology, sociology, anthropology, and economics. While these professors frequently produce scholarship that focuses on educational events, their orientation is one in which the goal is as often to enrich theory in their core disciplines as to effect improvement in the schools, at least in any proximate sense.

Decisions of the type that teachers are expected to make are embedded in the particular circumstances in which they arise. The rhythm of the lesson at the moment matters, especially as it connects to other activities that day and week. The teacher must consider the consequences for the other students when she does or does not give turns to participate to those who do not usually join in class discussions. Fairness is important to her. She knows also that it is a value that children hold high. It is unlikely that in the one or two seconds in which she must make a decision about which student to call upon, all the possible relevant factors run through her mind. Certainly she doesn't canvas her memory for all the research that might bear on the matter. She must act, and she must act in a fashion that is attuned to context, that is responsible, and that is consistent with her beliefs about the professional she is and wants to be.

Scientific reasoning is one thing. Practical reasoning is somewhat different. Scientific reasoning aims for the universal, practical reasoning for the particular. Scientific reasoning is abstract, practical reasoning concrete. Scientific reasoning is geared toward identifying the timeless principle, practical reasoning toward the timely. The goal of scientific reasoning is to understand, practical reasoning to act. As with all practical activities, teaching entails consideration of what is prudent, obligatory, and customary, what is feasible, efficient, and timely. These influences are highly localized and often poorly aligned with general knowledge about teaching and learning.

Case Studies

Research styles are being developed in education that are more holistic and interpretive. Case study research and the increased investment in evaluation of educational programs are examples of newer styles of inquiry in education that seem to have greater fidelity to educational practice than more conventional social science styles. To probe a question such as "What are (and might be) the aims of science education?" or "What are the outcomes of an experimental program to increase the interests of girls in science?" requires research tools that assist in understanding the philosophical underpinnings of the curriculum and the illumination of a range of perspectives about the program in question. Different people have different views depending on the results they want to maximize.

Case studies began to interest me during my association with the University of Illinois study that Bob Stake and Jack Easley conceived and the NSF supported in the late 1970s to ascertain the status of science, mathematics, and social studies education across the country. Twelve case studies were at the heart of the project. Unlike much prevailing research that aimed to influence practice, case studies required that educational activity be seen in context. They were a way to supplement other methods that were more remote from the details of classroom life. Case studies also opened the possibility for greater prominence to the view from the classroom, a feature absent in much of what I saw my university colleagues doing. Case studies involved intensive, direct observation of the events being examined. They usually required in-depth interviews with some of the participants; hence many viewpoints were highlighted. Documents specific to the research site were studied (courses of study, teacher journals, student work, for example).

I was ready to believe that such methods permit researchers to secure data about a situation obtainable in few other ways, and that such methods had a level of detail and verisimilitude rarely present in the experimental or other discipline-derived research studies that I had occasion to read or see. Case studies, indeed, turned out to be the method of choice in the OECD study of innovations in science, mathematics, and technology education for which Paul and I co-chaired the steering committee during the mid-1990s.

Leading the way in this trend toward the singular has been research in education evaluation. Drawing somewhat from the participant-observation tradition in social anthropology, but in many ways going beyond it, evaluators studied what students and teachers were doing in the classroom. They spent long periods of time examining a single school or teacher. There began to be less emphasis on controlled comparison and more on understanding the contexts in which educational events took place. As with the Mills College evaluation cited in chapter 5, such studies tended to explore events of interest to understand them more deeply, rather than necessarily to make definitive statements about how one educational approach compares with another. There is more narrative in educational scholarship today: stories (sometimes by the teachers and the students) that provide personal (and often ambiguous) portrayals of life in classrooms in attempts better to understand what goes on there. (Witness this volume!) There also has been more research by the teachers themselves, who are trying to get better at their work and who believe they can understand more about their own practices by examining it systematically. Some work in this genre is conducted in collaboration with other colleagues, as will be noted in the next chapter.

A safe generalization about education research is that there is less methodological orthodoxy in the early 21st century than there was in the 20th. The American Educational Research Association, an organization of researchers that attracts about 10,000 members to its annual meetings, includes virtually every variety of educational scholarship: experimental research, surveys, case studies, evaluations, historical inquiry, philosophical analysis, biographies, and much more—all done by people with a range of disciplinary and experiential backgrounds. This growing methodological pluralism is accompanied increasingly by a level of tolerance of differing views that few would have predicted 20 years earlier. The extraordinarily varied annual convention program of the American Educational Research Association is one indicator of a new pluralism. Another is the way faculty members at, say, the Stanford University School of Education tend to take each other's ideas more seriously than was the case only a decade or two ago, even when the orientation to research comes from entirely different intellectual traditions. They are learning to detect intellectual rigor in a variety of scholarly styles and toleration has increasingly led to respect. For those familiar with the intensity of methodological wars in academia, such an outcome would have seemed unlikely.

PAUL'S STORIES

Research and the Faculty Pecking Order

In my early acquaintance with university faculties of education, I saw that research had a strange location in their structure. Their bread and butter depended mainly on recent graduates being trained in one-year courses for the Postgraduate Certificate of Education that qualified them for secondary teaching. Up until the 1970s, such courses had two main elements: first the training in classroom methods in their specialist subjects, and secondly the academic study of so-called "disciplines of education," which were presented by formal lecture courses and examined by written papers. Staff who did the practical training did not have time for research, whilst those who taught theoretical courses did have time, but found their research identities within such disciplines as the history, or philosophy, or psychology, or sociology, of education. The "discipline" staff had publishing records and occupied the senior posts, although their research, being located in separate disciplines, usually bore little relevance to the complex problems of practice in schools. The "methods" staff tended to be a lower form of life. The students found the theoretical parts of their courses and the examination requirements irrelevant to their immediate concerns with survival in the classroom, which were only addressed in the practical component.

One attraction of my move in 1976 to Chelsea College to be head of their Centre for Science Education was that it was radically new in two ways. The subject methods staff, recruited from outstanding schoolteachers who had expanded their visions and experience by work in Nuffield curriculum projects, had comparable status to staff recruited from backgrounds in psychology, history, and philosophy. My predecessor, Kevin Keohane, had also been a professor of physics: He had moved to become the first professor of science education in the United Kingdom. He had also established our first chair in mathematics education. A third chair was held by a biology educator, and a fourth by a social historian who shared the vision of a cross-disciplinary approach to the problems of school education. The teacher training course was radically new in its focus on curriculum and school-based issues. There were no courses of the traditional type in the separate disciplines, and no written examinations. The teaching in the subject methods, together with the school practice training, was supplemented by reflective work that brought insights from several disciplines to bear on issues that the students would meet in school.

It was no mean feat that Kevin Keohane had convinced the government to fund this new department and had also secured, for its unconventional course, the academic validation of the federal University of London, which was essential to guarantee recognition of its qualification certificates. However, whilst the Chelsea department had succeeded by 1976 in establishing an excellent course with a good reputation in the schools, notably in London, the establishment of a broader academic presence was still a problem. There were successful M.A. courses, and a growing number of Ph.D. students. However, most of the staff did not have Ph.D.s, and the publication output, whilst being strong in the practical products of curriculum development, was thin in the recognised areas of educational research. The common practice for educational faculties of pursuing their research in the separate disciplines was neither feasible nor acceptable at Chelsea. The way forward was to move from curriculum development to in-depth exploration of the problems that such development was sure to encounter. Research had to be applicable and had to be focused on the learning of particular school subjects. However, clear models or precedents for such work were hard to find: Both the institution and its members were searching to invent their research identity.

The challenge, when I became director at Chelsea, to give priority to strengthening its research work was peculiarly difficult for me: I came to the task with long experience of research in physics, some experience of attempts to evaluate curriculum development, some involvement in the research of an examining authority, and work on a steering group for projects in the Birmingham faculty of education. My only systematic training had occurred before 1976 in joint research with two Chelsea staff, Jon Ogborn and Joan Bliss, exploring the reactions of physics undergraduates to their courses. I was initiated into techniques of interviewing and into methods of analysing interview transcripts. All of this hardly amounted to a training in conduct of research, let alone in directing it.

As I came to know the developing interests of my new colleagues, I was daunted by the wide range of methods that were being called into play. As these were drawn from many disciplines, the whole field seemed to be an interdisciplinary jungle. I remarked to Jon Ogborn that I had to be a jack-of-all-trades, but he pointed out that the rest of the catchphrase "and master of none," wouldn't do. It had to be master of all.

There Is No Right Answer, There Is Not Even Agreement on the Question

Prior to my arrival, the Chelsea department had secured substantial funding for a project on how learners develop understanding in secondary school mathematics and science. The original scheme for a unified approach across these two subjects had broken down. The mathematicians had embarked on an empirical study to chart the successes and failures of pupils as they tried to make progress in mathematics. This strand of work was free of controversy and produced remarkable results. One outstanding finding was that the range in the understanding of mathematical ideas across a typical group of 12-year olds was about the same as the progression in understanding of the average child over a period of about seven years. The project's results were both influential in policy debates and laid the basis for an ensuing succession of projects that continues to this day at King's College.

The science group had taken a different route, basing their work on Piaget's finding that there are distinct stages in mental development that occur in fixed sequence, with pupils developing the capacity to learn about increasingly more complex ideas as they progress from one stage to the next. The aim then was to find ways to describe the norms of such development across the school population so that science curricula could be matched to the development in time of pupils' innate capacities. On the one hand, the work attracted much attention and produced guidance for teachers that was widely welcomed. However, psychologists criticised the approach, some claiming that it was based on a misunderstanding of Piaget's theory, others that the theory was itself seriously flawed. I found the controversies, and the policy decisions entailed, hard to handle, not only because they involved personal tensions between colleagues at Chelsea, but also because I was not clear whether or not there could be any clear basis for deciding who was "right." As a physicist, I had been accustomed to controversy about the interpretations of established theories, or about how data might be interpreted in the light of these theories. Here I had to learn that different theories offered different perspectives on a complex social problem rather than an occasion for arm-wrestling to determine which was strongest. Whilst the paradigm clashes that Thomas Kuhn described might only flare up once per century in the natural sciences, in my new area they seemed to be ongoing bush fires.

As it turned out, this science work grounded in Piaget's theories also evolved over the years, and it exhibits to this day an enduring paradox. It has gained remarkable success in generating practical programmes for developing pupils' thinking skills, whilst there is at the same time continuing disagreement amongst psychologists about the theoretical explanation of its success.

Developing the Research Culture

Perspectives changed in 1985 when, on the merger of Chelsea College with King's College, my department had to merge with the King's faculty of education, a smaller multisubject group but one with a much longer history. As the new head of the expanded King's faculty, I met severe problems in managing the personal fears and conflicts amongst many faculty as each of the partner groups played out insecurities about losing out to the "other side." Research issues were part of this, not least because the King's faculty had been entrenched in the old-style divide between scholars in the "disciplines" and practitioners in the school subjects. So the faculty had to struggle once more with the problem of developing serious orientation in research for staff who had been appointed as experts in the practicalities of teacher training.

Matters slowly improved, and I escaped the pressures in 1989 when I resigned as department head and was replaced as head of the faculty by my colleague Arthur Lucas. He promptly asked me to establish a faculty research committee. One of its most rewarding initiatives was to set up a formal procedure for appraisal of research proposals, which had to be followed before any proposal could be submitted to an outside agency. All staff were encouraged to study any new proposal and then meet to form an interrogation panel, before which its authors had to defend it. In addition to helping to improve any proposal, this process was as useful as training for the critics as it was for the defenders. Later experience in appraising grant proposals as an external referee convinced me of the need for these internal appraisals.

These changes, together with some very fortunate new appointments, served to raise the research quality at King's, so that from 1990 onward it became one of only two top-rated research departments in education in the United Kingdom. However, the dependence of funding on external appraisals was placing increasing pressure on departments to "perform." Staff who were unproductive in placing research papers in refereed journals and who did not help earn research grants were clearly letting their colleagues down. Of particular concern were the rules, in that criteria biased toward pure research threatened the fragile interface between research and development. More recently, these rules have been altered to reduce the "pure" bias.

Going Personal

My own research identity was still cloudy. By contrast with physics research, where there was so firm a consensus about the epistemology and the methodology that these were hardly ever discussed, educational research seemed to be somewhere between a jungle, with luxuriant growth weak in fibrous strength, and a desert, arid in providing little useful guidance for practitioners. Studies of the fate of curriculum initiatives, notably those of Stake and Easley at the University of Illinois, were exposing the ways in which innovations might readily founder on the rocks of the inevitable difficulties that teachers faced in changing their practice; their capacity to do this had been too lightly taken for granted.

Adding to this problem of relevance and applicability was a concern about my own lack of a clear theoretical base in the work that I had done. I suspected that the prevalence, in my personal portfolio of empirical work underpinned by makeshift theories derived largely by induction, was a sign of the amateur. The comfort was that maybe I was facing the inevitable underlying problems of a complex field where the notion of "theory" is problematic.

This fuzziness in research identity did not follow from any failure with significant funded projects; some of the successes in these are described in other chapters. Perhaps the least fuzzy of these was the project in primary science discussed in chapter 2, because here was a research programme in line with current paradigms and concerns, yet oriented toward practical application, first in curriculum development, and then in teacher development as part of dissemination. Recently it is coming full circle: A team headed by Patricia Murphy at the Open University has been studying in detail the classroom work of selected teachers who are known to be successful in producing progress in their pupils' thinking. The aim is to learn from practitioners about effective ways of advancing pupils' understanding of science concepts.

The lesson that classroom success depends on teachers' beliefs about and confidence in the teaching of science emerged clearly in another project that started from the view that our earlier primary science concepts research lacked the fine grain and the depth needed to give us adequate picture of the progress of individual pupils' understanding. A group at King's secured a grant to support work in which we looked in detail at a single topic in science, using the methods of qualitative research to study the development, with age, of pupils' understanding of one particular topic— forces in equilibrium. We aimed to develop a systematic description of the ways in which this understanding was actually achieved by pupils (Black et al., 1994). The approach was basically constructivist in focusing on pupils' responses in interviews to carefully selected phenomena, these responses being analysed in the light of the conceptual goals that constituted the accepted scientific view. One difficulty was that for this, albeit quite elementary, topic, many textbooks and other advisory materials for teachers were confusingly inaccurate in their explanation of the concepts. Those teachers who were minded to study and then use advisory material based on our results (Simon et al., 1994) reported that this material was more clear and informative than anything they had previously encountered. The irony was that if relevance depended on such detailed study, then the total time needed for teachers to study the results in this depth for every topic made the approach impracticable.

There was another significant outcome. When I along with others was consulted about revision of the national science curriculum, we were able to point out both from this work and from our earlier primary science research that certain topics were too demanding for the age ranges to which they were assigned, and to suggest that they either be moved or replaced by wording to represent simpler starting targets.

The Numbers Matter

One of the main attractions of academic research is the opportunity to work with gifted research students. Apart from the reward of seeing them develop under one's guidance, one also learns from their work. My outstanding example was Jo Boaler: She achieved far more than merely adding value to any ideas of mine, as her subsequently successful career has shown. However, when her doctoral thesis subsequently won a prize for one of the best of its year, and the book that was based on it then won another prize for the best educational book of its year (Boaler, 1997), I was able to bask in reflected glory. But what gave me particular pleasure was a comment by a fellow professor at King's, Stephen Ball, one well versed in ethnographic research methods and a leading figure in the sociology of education, when he helped to appraise her work as part of our system of monitoring progress of doctoral students. He remarked that he was impressed by the power of her combination, one rarely found, of qualitative data with quantitative measures. I was well aware that many researchers in education not only chose qualitative rather than quantitative approaches in their own work, but also argued that quantitative data could yield little useful insight. The dual approach that I had influenced Jo to adopt followed my own conviction that a combination of paradigms, rather than a contest between them, would be particularly productive. The impact of her book owed something to the appeal of the quantitative data, for one of its many lessons was that it showed through test scores that pupils taught by progressive methods did learn effectively by comparison with those in traditional classrooms.

Research Can Influence Practice

Problems about the relevance of research results were brought home to me in a new way by a revival of my interest in classroom formative assessment, which had originally been stimulated the work of TGAT, described in chapter 5. Shortly after my formal retirement in 1995, I was invited by an assessment study group of the British Educational Research Association to carry out a review of the literature on formative assessment. Since this offered me the prospect of financial and collegial support for something that I wanted to do anyway, I was happy to accept. The one condition that I made, that I should do the work jointly with my colleague Dylan Wiliam at King's, was readily agreed, and this has turned out to be a far wiser move than I could have anticipated.

The work took much of my time for the next 15 months, and, with help and advice en route from the BERA group, we brought it to a conclusion with two publications early in 1998. The first was a 70-page review article surveying the work of about 250 published papers drawn from a wide variety of journals (Black & Wiliam, 1998a). Two main lessons emerged. One was that a variety of studies had produced quantitative evidence that initiatives to develop classroom formative assessment could produce remarkable learning gains. The second was that assembled together, the diverse literature contained many ideas about the conduct and implications of work of this type.

All of this confirmed previous beliefs to an extent that far exceeded my expectations, and I was profoundly grateful to have a critical and constructive fellow author to help ensure that my prejudices had not distorted my judgment. This confidence was further confirmed when the article appeared because the journal editor, Patricia Broadfoot, who had also been a member of the BERA group, had invited seven experts from around the world to write papers in response to our article. Whilst these added a great deal to thinking in the field, none of them queried the main findings.

The second publication arose because the cogency of the evidence inspired Dylan and myself, and the BERA group, to want to give the main message wider publicity. So we wrote a 20-page booklet entitled "Inside the Black Box" (Black & Wiliam, 1998b). The "black box" was the classroom, and we highlighted this because the message was that standards could best be raised by nurturing the quality of the work of teachers in the classroom rather than by the common means, beloved by politicians, of imposing rules, evaluations, and sanctions from outside it. The booklet spelt out the main findings of our review, but went on to say that there did not and could not follow from this any simple recipes to improve teaching. The belief that we set out was that research results such as the ones that we had assembled could not in any simple sense be applied to practice. The context and person of the teacher were all important, so we called for patient development work in which teachers could draw upon the research lessons as stimuli or provocations that would both encourage and support them in inventing new knowledge about pedagogy as they transformed the ideas into workable practices.

We achieved some media publicity on releasing the booklet. A high point was when I was attacked by name in an editorial in the *London Times* for asserting that the competitive outlook engendered by the giving of marks and grades could be harmful to learning. The newspaper's argument was that it was a hard, competitive world and pupils had to be prepared for it. I might have replied by commenting on the social ideology that underpinned such a view but chose the more limited response of quoting the research evidence that any such preparation had actually reduced pupils' learning achievements. The subsequent popularity of this booklet took us by surprise. Although it can only be obtained by direct request to King's College, about 18,000 copies had been sold within three years, and an American version was also published (Black & Wiliam, 1998c). Since its publication, Dylan and I have received numerous requests to address meetings of teachers, and all have expressed positive support for the message. Many schools and local authority districts are now incorporating formative assessment into their plans for professional development, and the term "assessment for learning" is now featured in government programs for improving pupils' achievements.

So we wonder: Why did a message based on research evidence have such an impact at a time when there was controversy about the uselessness of such research? A possible answer is the evident appeal of the quantitative evidence, that pupils really do achieve higher test scores. A related factor has been expressed to us by many teachers in the form "We have always believed that this was true, it is heartening to see evidence that we were right." This leads to a third possibility, which is that the profession, overburdened and demoralised by repeated impositions of external rules, were heartened to see a strong argument that what really mattered was support for their activities inside their classrooms. Finally, our emphasis that we had no recipe but that it was for teachers themselves to work out how to transform the ideas into working practice recognised their dignity by making clear that their own professionalism was the main key to the quest of politicians and the public for the raising of standards.

This academic study of formative assessment led us to pursue work with teachers on the application of the ideas. This will be described in chapter 7.

JOINT REFLECTIONS ABOUT RESEARCH AND PRACTICE

In 1968, Joseph Schwab of the University of Chicago addressed the curriculum division of the AERA and later published a paper based on the talk (Schwab, 1969). Schwab was a professor of natural science and of education. He had worked during the 1960s in the Biological Sciences Curriculum Study, one of the early projects funded by the NSF to change the science curriculum. He contended, based partly on his experiences in the biology project, that the field of curriculum study was moribund. It relies on theory in an area where theory is inappropriate, he said. What is needed is a discipline not focused on the theoretical but instead on choice and action. He maintained, further, that research should converge on the "enduring problems of education," rather than on the tenets of the presumed parent disciplines. He asserted that one facet of a *practical* perspective on education is the "anticipatory generation of alternatives," and that empirical study in classrooms be undertaken not to address theoretical concerns, but to begin "to know what we are doing."

Deliberation is at the heart of practical inquiry, he asserted, rather than induction or deduction. Its goal is the crafting of defensible action, and it deals with both ends and means, which must be treated "as mutually determining one another." To move toward this kind of research, Schwab envisioned a weakening of the boundaries that "separate psychologist from philosopher, sociologist from test constructor, historian from administrator." Also, he asserted, it would have to include teachers, supervisors, and school administrators.

At many levels, the fact that researchers from diverse fields are engaging collaboratively in developing educational improvements is heartening. It is much more common today than in 1969 for university professors in a range of fields from anthropology to zoology to be collaborating with teachers and school administrators in the conduct of research. There are more journals than there were in the 1960s that publish the results of such inquiry. More teachers today than in the 1960s report their research activities at scholarly conferences. Collaborative ventures involving university-based researchers and those in the schools are encouraged by almost all funding agencies, including the NSF. Though there is a long way to go before the practicalities of teaching and school administration drive most university-level research in the field of education, the changes over the three decades are encouraging and probably would please Schwab; there is a pluralism in educational research that few would have predicted even 15 years ago.

In a related vein, battles about the worth of various types of research styles—experiments, narratives, evaluations, case studies—have been yielding to discussions about quality, regardless of genre. In 2001, the National Research Council's *ad hoc* Committee on Scientific Principles in Educational Research published a report titled *Science, Evidence, and Inference in Education* as the initial document in a longer study titled

Scientific Research in Education (2002). The NRC's credibility resides in its standing as the embodiment of the scientific community. The committee suggested that in its future work it "should distinguish between science as an act of inquiry and science as an act of design." In the report, "inquiry" corresponds roughly to canonically familiar scientific research, wherein the goal is to produce new generalizable knowledge. "Design" is focused on practical approaches to concrete problems and challenges; it relies heavily on local knowledge and necessarily operates in highly particularized settings. Note that both inquiry and design in the report fall under a *science* rubric. The report states firmly that diversity of research styles is positive and that there is no one model of quality.

The work at Chelsea seems to have anticipated this move toward greater diversity in educational research. Much of the lead in the new unit went to people who came directly from fields of practice. The Chelsea staff, many from academia, accepted the challenge of trying to invent a research tradition, rather than having to transform one in which they were already immersed. Those who approached matters empirically, and brought to bear on them their subject knowledge and their experience of teaching, were able to make important contributions, though there were problems when it came to generalizing the results. The Chelsea group learned, as Schwab anticipated, that it was a far different matter to diagnose problems in education than it was to devise ways to overcome them.

Our Conclusions

It is evident that the many researches conducted on a narrow basis have much to offer. Given, for example, the predilections of policymakers and the public for the tidily quantifiable, results of this type can be valuable in arousing and directing concern in helpful ways. But any such contribution can be counterproductive if it is accepted on an assumption that the application of research findings is a straightforward matter. Findings of this type have to be reconstructed to transform them into practitioner knowledge. This task is far from being a trivial final stage of the preceding research, and it has to be done by those engaged in the struggles of providing educational services directly to children: teachers and school administrators.

The problems that educational research is trying to address are complex, mostly local, and embedded in context. Insights developed in one setting have to be reexamined for their relevance to another. The task is to try to develop understanding of a highly individualized and personal relationship between teacher and student, one in which the values and the moral engagement of the teacher, and the developing and often fragile persona of each student, are paramount. Narratives and case studies may be more helpful than systematic frameworks that strive for generalizable principles. The Ph.D. thesis presented as a novel is not an absurd idea if it sheds light on an enduring educational issue—although only a rare and courageous genius would be well advised to try it.

7

Teachers

The central element in improving education, of course, is the teacher and how she is viewed in the process of educational change. Is the teacher a person who adapts a curriculum developed by other kinds of experts to the needs of the students she teaches? In that case, she is not necessarily involved in initiating new programs, though her insights are sought about matters like feasibility and instructional approaches. Is she a person who joins directly in conceptualizing the innovation, drawing on her knowledge of the content-related needs of her students? In that case, she shares with experts in the various fields of science the authority and responsibility of choosing topics that seem most salient. To what degree do teachers collectively and collaboratively take responsibility for designing the curriculum? If the level of such involvement is significant, what kinds of opportunities are created for teachers to deliberate about such matters?

MIKE'S STORIES

The Advantages of Sink or Swim

When I started teaching in a high school in New York City in 1948, I had little guidance from either the administration of the school or the authorities at the state level either about what or how to teach. The choice of topics and textbooks was mine—so too were the methods of instruction. This pattern of benign inattentiveness continued when I went to the suburbs after two years to teach in elementary schools.

The general condition of science teaching was as varied as the communities in which it occurred, the hopes and expectations of the parents, and the predilections of the individual teachers. Some schools emphasized the kind of academic achievement that seemed most closely related to college admission and success. Others valued the kinds of skills associated with gainful employment on graduation. A large number placed highest priority on keeping students from dropping out of school.

At the high school where I taught, parents expected their children to go to college upon graduation. Almost all of them did. An important element in decisions about college admission was the score students received on statewide, standardized examinations developed by the State of New York Board of Regents. These tests, by subjects, were given at the same time at every high school in New York. Thus every student finishing a one-year first course in biology took an identical test at the same time. Each examination took three hours—clearly a serious and consequential commitment. How, then, could the school in which I taught accord me latitude about topics to emphasize, laboratory activities to design, and textbooks to choose?

The short answer is that I reserved about a month at the end of the school year to coach the students on the nature of the Regents Examination and how to pass it. During those weeks, we did almost nothing but review past Regents Examinations. They, and past exams in all Regents subjects, were available for a modest price at bookstores. Up to the beginning of the Regents review, I might have spent a month on genetics, a month on body systems, a month on comparative anatomy, and/or a month on evolution. At the time, I was particularly interested in ecology and conservation, and so my students and I spent significant periods of time in Manhattan's Central Park studying relationships among various species, and learning something, too, about local geological formations. I was interested also in how biology relates to various social and personal issues, like protection of agricultural lands and maintenance of individual and community health. It was my impression that other teachers in the state also followed their professionally related individual priorities, though the amount of time reserved for coaching for the exam depended on the teacher's priorities and the capabilities of the students. The point is that teachers had discretion about topics that would be studied by the students. The influence of the Regents Examination was powerful, but not total.

In addition to being able to feature my own preferences in my classes, I was able to capitalize on the interests of the students. When there was a water shortage in the city of New York and the public was being urged to use water sparingly, I altered the curriculum in my General Science course for ninth graders to focus on New York's system for obtaining water from watersheds and reservoirs upstate, weather patterns that had resulted in below-normal rainfall, increasing rates of usage, and water purification methods employed by the city. Since newspapers and radio were devoting considerable attention to the topic, it was one of more than passing interest to the students and their parents.

The fact that I was able to exercise personal judgment about what and how to teach was one of the most attractive features of my new job as teacher. Like everyone, I knew more about some subjects than others. I wasn't particularly strong in genetics, beyond the rudiments. It surely is the case that my students did not learn as much about the subject as their friends who studied with someone with greater knowledge. On the other hand, those in my classes learned some other topics in greater depth, like evolution, and probably learned them better because their teacher was deeply interested and better informed. Furthermore, I had been through a teacher education program that emphasized the importance of the relevance of science content to the lives of students and their communities, a viewpoint I embraced. So I was pleased professionally that I could work in a setting that helped me accent my own priorities and become the kind of teacher I wanted to be.

Advancing a Litmus Test for Education Policy

The importance of these kinds of satisfactions came to loom large in my outlook toward the improvement of science education. My short stint at the NSF in 1986 as senior advisor provided an opportunity to reacquaint myself with issues and people in science education. The NSF had programs in curriculum, teacher education, and education research. I began to press the view that a primary test by which new initiatives for NSF programs should be judged was whether or not they were more or less likely to improve the quality of science teachers, and particularly whether they enhanced the occupation of science teaching so as to attract and retain the country's most able people. Nothing, I came increasingly to believe, was as important to the quality of science education as the capabilities of those who choose to teach—and I had become convinced that many education initiatives intended to improve education quality were counterproductive.

Examples were not difficult to find. By the mid-1980s, there had been a spate of "minimum competency" legislation enacted by states across the country. In one form, students could not receive a high school diploma unless they passed specially devised state-level examinations. Much of the voiced objection to the eventual result was that racial and ethnic minorities fared less well than others. But there were curriculum consequences as well. It was not difficult to predict that examinations with such high stakes for students would lead to a narrowing of the schools' programs: Those subjects and topics for which student achievement could be most readily assessed with existing testing technology would be emphasized, while those that did not lend themselves to such examination methods would fade.

Unintended Consequences

Such an outcome was foreseeable, and foreseen. Matthew Arnold, as he visited schools all over England more than 100 years before as a school inspector, warned that a countrywide assessment scheme that has been put into place would lead to an undesirable narrowing of the curriculum. He was concerned that the arts, literature, and humanistic studies, in particular, would atrophy. (The system under which he was operating, called "payment by results," even tied financial allocations to test scores, a system frequently advocated in the United States today, even by some Presidents.) Approaches to science education that were not readily assessed by relatively inexpensive tests that called only for multiple-choice or short-answer responses would be neglected, I believed. If a goal of science education were to teach students to design and carry out an experiment, it would not likely be taken seriously unless it appeared on the examination. And it was deemed simply too expensive to measure such an outcome in all the students who would be required to take the test. Besides, the experts weren't sure how to make the assessment.

What was less obvious to me, but turned out to be the case, was that minimum competency legislation would lead to a leveling of the curriculum—but not solely a leveling up, which was its purpose, but a leveling *down* as well. Here's how it worked: Every school was faced with the necessity of assuring that as many students as possible would graduate. The tests that were devised made the specific goals for the science curriculum clear. Sample questions were distributed, so everyone knew the kinds of questions that would be asked. Not unreasonably, available resources were redirected within each school to try to assure that students achieving at only marginal levels would pass. So far, so good.

But where did the resources come from? From instructional resources that previously had been assigned to students whose achievement was not judged to be a problem. For example, advanced classes in science and mathematics were dropped in many high schools in California, so teachers could spend their time with students who needed help in passing the state-level examinations. Furthermore, the topics to be taught in the remaining classes were constrained by the focus of the examinations, thus significantly limiting the latitude teachers would have in choosing content: She could less easily go into depth in topics that arose somewhat unexpectedly and that seemed important. She was less able to pick up on subject matter in which students seemed particularly interested. She could not spend more generous amounts of time on issues about which she was specially knowledgeable.

The more science teaching tended to be scripted by agencies outside the school, such as legislatures and producers of educational tests, the less opportunity there was for teachers to play to their strengths and interests. One purpose, indeed, is to make sure everyone at least gets certain things "right." But the less teachers are able to play to their strengths and interests, the less effective they are likely to be with students. At least as important, the less satisfying teaching is likely to be as a lifetime career. It is by now well known that people who are able to exercise levels of discretion in fulfilling their responsibilities are able to accomplish more. The principle is well established in business and industry, even, increasingly, in government.

Many attempts to improve education stem from people and agencies outside the education system and seem driven by the view that schools and teachers must be "reformed." The actions taken to assure improvement almost always are narrowing—not only in terms of the teacher's vision but also with respect to curriculum. Sometimes teaching methods are targeted as well. (Don't use a language other than English. Teach phonics so that children can learn to read.) The intent and substance of such directives are not lost on teachers. Neither is the tone, which often sounds punitive. They, the teachers, are the problem. And since the new demands inevitably fall on all the teachers, all the teachers take the blame and the consequences. Once receiving that message, the choice of leaving the profession becomes more attractive—for all teachers, but particularly for those who have the option. Since those who can leave are often the teachers who are best qualified, the initiatives intended to improve the quality of curriculum and teaching have perverse and counterproductive effects. Legislation and administrative regulations are very blunt instruments for improving individualized, personal services such as education. The saddest part is that so many of the detrimental effects are entirely predictable.

National Science Education Standards and Teacher Quality: More on Unintended Consequences

I saw the movement to establish national standards for mathematics and science education in the early 1990s as having the same potential for negative and undesired side effects. In the case of mathematics, I had found it encouraging that standards development had been undertaken nationally by the National Council for Teachers of Mathematics (NCTM, 1989), the largest and most influential organization of mathematics teachers. While the resulting standards initially garnered the support of a broad spectrum of mathematicians as well as mathematics educators, I knew that teachers had been centrally involved in their development. This fact was an encouraging indication that the standards might be received well in the classroom and be viewed as constructive by the teachers; teachers would be less likely to believe that the initiative was just one more example of powerful people outside schools and classroom exercising a penchant for remote control of their professional practices.

There was lots of pressure to develop national standards for science education. The first President Bush had convened an education summit in 1989 that included the governors of all 50 states. A resulting declaration stated several broad goals for the improvement of education, among them:

> By the year 2000, American students will leave grades four, eight, and twelve having demonstrated competency in challenging subject matter including English, mathematics, science, history, and geography. . . . U.S. students will be first in the world in science and mathematics achievement. (U.S. Department of Education, 1989)

With the NCTM Standards as a model, the Secretary of Education in a document prepared for the President in 1991 declared,

> New World Standards: Standards will be developed. . . for each of the five core subject areas that represent what young Americans need to know and be able to do if they are to live and work successfully in today's world. These standards will incorporate both knowledge and skills, to ensure that, when they leave school, young Americans are prepared for further study and the work force. (U.S. Department of Education, 1991)

In 1992, a grant was awarded to the National Research Council (NRC) of the National Academy of Sciences to develop standards. I was among those asked to serve on the large National Committee for Science Education Standards and Assessment, the group that would provide direction for the overall effort. But I was dubious about accepting because, unlike the NCTM Standards, the project did not have the stamp of classroom teachers. Though a few teachers would be on the committee, the effort had the potential for being one more effort at trying to mold classroom practice from afar. Teachers would be told what to teach, but not necessarily with much understanding or support. Nevertheless, I consented to join.

It turned out that I was not alone in my skepticism. At the inaugural meeting of the committee, within the first hour in fact, several of us voiced misgivings. Some members had reservations in principle. They said that a certain amount of variation in the science curriculum was desirable to meet local circumstances and needs. Standards could go too far toward standardization and rob local school districts of discretionary authority. The committee chair and some of the staff present responded that standards developed by the NRC necessarily would be voluntary because it had no authority to assure that they were followed.

Other members spoke forcefully to the point that standards had the potential for further teacher bashing. Goals would be articulated. However laudable they might be in conceptualizing a desirable program of science education, however, teachers likely would be blamed if the standards were not met, regardless of their own culpability. What if they did not have the physical resources, the space, or the equipment needed to carry out a desirable program? What if they had not received the kind of education necessary to adhere to the standards? What if the tests given to their students did not comport with the pedagogical styles and content that the standards would stipulate?

The discussion was intense. The NRC staff listened carefully. There seemed to be consensus. In the end, it was decided that standards would be developed not only in subject matter content, which had been the call of the Secretary of Education, but, separately, in teaching, in professional development of teachers, and in assessment. Additionally, standards were developed for programs and the support needed for the entire system. One Program Standard that appeared in the final document states, "The science program should be coordinated with the mathematics program to enhance student use of mathematics in the study of science and to improve student understanding of mathematics" (National Research Council, 1996, p. 214). A System Standard stipulates, "Policies must be supported with resources" (p. 232). Another states, "All policy instruments must be reviewed for possible unintended effects on the classroom practice of science education" (pp. 232, 233). Among many highlighted statements in the section on Teaching Standards, the document emphasizes that teachers should "encourage and model the skills of scientific inquiry, as well as the curiosity, openness to new ideas, and skepticism that characterize science" (p. 37). For Professional Development, ". . . activities must provide regular, frequent opportunities for individual and collegial examination and reflection on classroom and instructional practice" and "provide opportunities for teachers to receive feedback about their teaching and to understand, analyze, and apply that feedback to improve practice" (p. 68). The first Assessment Standard states, "Assessments must be consistent with the decisions they are designed to inform," and "The relationship between the decisions and the data is clear" (p. 78).

The view of standards for elementary and secondary schools projected by the National Academy of Sciences is far from traditional. Thus standards were promulgated with the intention of highlighting the fact that improving educational quality, though most directly a responsibility of

teachers, is not theirs alone. Serious attention to all dimensions of the educational system is a requirement for progress. Teacher education has to be
reexamined, along with the appropriateness of the examination system, for
example. The final version of the *Standards* had at least the potential for
advancing the field by fostering cooperation among a broad range of actors
on the science education scene. Shared responsibility by several groups may
make it more possible for everyone to take credit—and discourage blaming
any one of them for lack of success. Not least, it is clear from the *Standards*
that public funds must be appropriated for the purpose. Improving educational quality cannot be done on the cheap.

Teachers and Curriculum Development: Bottom-Up Preferences, Again

Frequently the need for curriculum development arises at the school level
and necessitates strong involvement by teachers. A new state framework
for science is released, a sort of standards-like document that outlines in
broad and general terms what schools of the state are expected to teach.
But the statements of content to be included are general. Teachers at district and site level must work out what the implications are in the classroom. In most American school districts, time is allocated for teachers to
fulfill this responsibility, although considerable amounts of additional time
are almost always required.

In the case of small districts, the task might be regional. When
California secondary schools moved toward "integrated" science in the
early 1990s (chapter 2), ten "hubs" were established around the state
where teachers met to discuss what it meant to move from a subject-by-
subject approach—usually general science or earth science, followed by
biology, followed by chemistry, followed by physics—to one in which these
subjects would be taught in some connected fashion. The State Department
of Education exercised little control over the emerging curriculum. The
department's role was one of coordination, whereby it facilitated communication among the hubs to enable teachers at one hub to learn about what
was happening at the others.

In many ways, it was a teacher-led initiative. The state had provided
guidelines in the form of a framework that teachers along with scientists
from the universities had participated in creating. Teachers created the
operational curriculum. As might be expected in a large state like
California, there was considerable variability among the hubs. Some coordinated the science offerings more than integrating them. That is, the chemistry component might emphasize solutions while the earth science component considered leaching of soils. In some places, there was solely alterna-
tion of topics—one from chemistry, followed by one from physics, fol-

lowed by one from biology.

An unfamiliar challenge faced the admissions committee of the University of California that determined requirements for all eight campuses that taught undergraduates. How should it handle this curriculum innovation in deciding whether students from the high schools met the admissions requirement of at least two years of laboratory science? If the university did not approve the concept, the schools would certainly revert to a subject-by-subject sequence, thus vitiating the new framework. The committee was accustomed to dealing with General Science, Biology, Earth Sciences, Chemistry, and Physics, but not with Integrated Science I, Integrated Science II, and Integrated Science III. No one yet knew what this general label meant, what the courses looked like in reality. Far from closing the door to this initiative from the high schools, however, the admissions committee decided to consider each high school's integrated science series as a unique set in university decisions about admission. Was there sufficient laboratory work? Were key science concepts taught? On a high-school-by-high-school basis, the admissions committee considered and acted upon the petitions from around the state to decide if that school's students met requirements for university entrance.

This practice is not very different from that employed in some other countries. Even in an educational system as centralized as Japan's, it is left to the 100-plus prefectures to figure out the actual classroom curriculum when the Ministry of Education issues a new course of study. Typically the prefecture, in turn, draws on the resources of the individual schools. When a new science curriculum for primary grades was released in 1989 from the Ministry of Education in Tokyo, Yokohama City created a committee to implement it locally. The committee was composed of about 60 members, with two or three from each elementary school. The school-level groups fed information to the larger committee and *vice versa*, in the process of creating the distinctive Yokohama City science curriculum. True, it looked only a bit different from the one in Kobe or Osaka, but the local teachers made decisions about how much time to spend on different topics, depending, in part, on the relevance of the subject matter to issues of concern in the local community.

Occasionally the process starts from the classroom. For the OECD project on innovations in science, mathematics, and technology education, Germany chose to study a project on integrated science in the state of Schlesweg-Holstein. It was an initiative that aimed to connect the science that students studied in school with matters of practical consequence in the community. The teachers believed that such a focus necessitated an integrated curriculum, one that drew on several disciplines to comprehend a practical matter such as the local uses and sources of water, for example.

The group of teachers approached professors in the science education center at the University of Kiel, and ultimately several of the university faculty collaborated with the teachers in translating their vision of a desirable curriculum into materials for students.

Mixed Messages

The science education policy scene internationally offers mixed messages about the extent to which teachers are viewed as central figures in curriculum development. On the one hand, it is recognized that no changes are likely to be deep or lasting unless teachers are committed to the new programs. It simply doesn't work to create a curriculum without participation by teachers and expect it to be implemented with fidelity. If pressed to hew to the curriculum from state or national authorities, teachers are unable to emphasize the content they know best—and all teachers (and scientists) know some topics better than others, and are better at teaching them. Furthermore, the more the curriculum departs from traditional pedagogical practices, the greater the difficulty, so teachers are accorded considerable latitude. In some other countries, on the other hand, particularly in the English-speaking world, teachers are viewed as a major reason for the questionable quality of education. They are accorded little respect or trust compared to teachers in most countries in Europe and Asia. To accord teachers the key responsibility for making the necessary changes is to perpetuate mediocrity, it is claimed. In these countries, and especially in the United States, high-stakes examinations are administered to students frequently, with school-level scores publicized widely—further increasing the pressure to conform to a tightly framed curriculum.

In the United States, it is often suggested that teacher certification requirements be dropped or modified to enable well-educated scientists to enter the profession. The intent here is to drop or drastically reduce courses in education—those on pedagogy, history and philosophy of education, and social and behavioral foundations of education. Some college science professors, a few of whom are distinguished in their respective fields and famous as teachers, are fond of pointing out that they would not be permitted to teach in the elementary and high schools because they lack the formal requirements in education. They are correct. Sometimes certification boards in individual states make it much easier for such people to obtain a temporary teaching license. The permanent one is contingent on successful experience in the classroom. All this may be well and good. But what if these presumably more qualified teachers are then constrained in what they teach by a highly prescriptive curriculum adopted by the state to assure minimum levels of achievement, one that doesn't permit them to teach to their own special strengths? Are they likely to remain in the classroom if they are unable to teach the topics they like and know best, if they are unable to exercise the kinds of latitude that they are accustomed to in their college courses?

Building on the Personal: How You Teach Depends on Who You Are

Virtually all of science education policy is directed toward improving what happens when teachers meet with students in the classroom. In the end, little else matters. Yet policymakers have never known what to make of teachers or how to deal with them. As noted, teachers are the weak link in the education system in the view of many. As such, they must be held accountable, so test them. Also test the students to learn what the teachers are or are not accomplishing. A major driving force behind the standards movement for many politicians is to provide benchmarks by which to gauge teacher competence.

But there is also a personal element in teaching, as there is in all realms of professional practice, that is both a central ingredient in quality and, at the same time, difficult to induce or reproduce through teacher preparation programs. Teachers, like other professionals, are people who stand for certain things and who exemplify attributes of character and personality that are intimately linked to and reflected in their practice. Often they are the teacher's most distinctive qualities, as all of us who have been students realize. Furthermore, each teacher who is remembered clearly elicits feelings of respect and warmth (or distaste and antipathy) for unique reasons. One favorite teacher is remembered for being especially passionate about her subject, another for her special way of encouraging students to do their best, another for her generosity in taking extra time with students who are having difficulties. There are many ways to be a good teacher, just as there are many ways to be a good parent, a good politician, a good physician, or a good engineer. In any profession, outstanding practitioners have special knowledge; they know and can employ the norms of best practice. But their success depends significantly on their personal qualities, like their dependability, their respect for the opinions of others, and their sense of fairness, among many others. In practical affairs, especially those in which one's actions affect other people, these characteristics are frequently paramount.

It was noted in the last chapter that researchers are coming to understand some of the distinctions between practical reasoning and most forms of scientific reasoning in their investigations of teaching in actual classrooms. As they do so, they are becoming increasingly sensitive to context and appreciative of the many and varying factors that influence individual teachers. The setting for a teacher's educational practice makes a difference: the nature of the students, the expectations of the parents, the curriculum guidelines that are employed, the teaching norms in the school—and, not least, the predilections of the teacher herself. New scholarship on "communities of practice," much of it from sociologists and anthropologists, emphasizes the degree to which one is influenced by peers. Many cognitive scientists have turned fresh attention to the importance of the "situation" in learning. In both of these scholarly perspectives, there is an emerging new focus on the teacher as a person and not solely as a member of a group. The concept of teacher identity is becoming more prominent in the research literature. It is being recognized that policies designed to improve education must somehow recognize and incorporate the fact that different teachers are driven by different conceptions of their work, that these conceptions are often deep, and that they have powerful influences on how any teacher changes her practices.

Practical Reasoning and Action Research

My own thinking about practical reasoning has been influenced most strongly by philosophies that go back at least to those enunciated more than 2,400 years ago by Aristotle. In the *Ethics*, Aristotle contrasts the quest for and knowledge of broad principles, *episteme* (which today we would call science), with practical wisdom, or *phronesis*. Practical reasoning is directed toward action, while scientific reasoning is directed toward understanding. The two are related, of course. One doesn't usually act well without knowledge. But one learns special things about one's practice (and oneself) when action is required. A teacher may believe, for example, that fairness to students is a preeminent value. She may question just what she means by fairness, however, when she actually sees herself treating some students quite differently from others where greater evenhandedness seems more appropriate.

My understanding of practical reasoning—and its emphasis in particular circumstances on what is prudent, what is timely, what is obligatory, what is personal, and what is moral—has led me to work with teachers in ways that I believe to be consonant with the settings in which they find themselves and the people they are and want to become. When I left the Stanford deanship and resumed more active direct involvement in research and teacher education, my philosophical predisposition led me to a form of teacher inquiry on their own practice called *action research*. Put simply, action research, at least the variety to which I am most attracted, emphasizes the centrality in professional development of teachers investigating their own practice by trying to change it, then discussing the results with other teachers who are trying to move in the same direction. This sort of research in classrooms is inevitably local and personal. What makes it research, if it is research, is that it is systematic and that it is criticized by a group of like-minded peers (Atkin, 1992).

Here's how the general approach to action research works for prospective science teachers in my classes (or teachers in nearby schools with whom I work): They first come to agree, for one kind of example, that they want students to be more actively involved in science work. They see many students as undesirably passive, doing what is required but little more. So the teachers talk about what might be the reasons. In discussion, the concept of ownership arises. Perhaps the students would participate more energetically if they had a stronger stake in what was happening in the classroom. What is ownership? How might it be enhanced? One teacher suggests that students be given the opportunity to help define the problem. Another suggests that they help design the experiment, or develop a data table. These ideas, and others like them, are discussed at length, then tried in the teachers' own classrooms. At their next meeting, perhaps a week later, the teachers compare results, and discuss what they might try next to further test their ideas. This emphasis on action in their own classrooms offers the opportunity to learn, with peers who share the same general goals, more about themselves and their distinctive approaches to teaching.

These kinds of deliberations among teachers are directed not so much toward deciding upon a single course of action that is best under all conditions, as toward what is defensible under the circumstances. There is no one best way for teachers to involve students in genuine scientific inquiry. It depends on evolving meanings of "involve" and "inquiry" that different teachers and students bring to the classroom and what they learn from their experiences. These meanings are deepened and honed by trying continually to improve, then reflecting on what was done and discussing the events and the consequences with sympathetic and critical colleagues. Actually, scientists work much the same way as they discuss their own work and develop their ideas. A difference is that scientists usually aim for universal and broadly applicable principles. Teachers engaged in action research strive for principled action in their own classrooms.

Action research of this sort seems to epitomize where my experiences and philosophy of education have taken me after sixty years. Action research emphasizes shared values among groups of practicing professionals, and it doesn't sacrifice the personal. It is practiced in a setting of broad professional consensus, without ignoring differences. It accents responsibility for what happens to students, while at the same time, through deliberation with others, making public the practices that demonstrate such responsibility.

Perhaps most of all, it accents the point that becoming the teacher one wants to be is a lifetime quest. After decades in the classroom, I still am not the teacher I want to be, and never will be. Being a teacher is less a process of reaching a particular destination than a matter of continually shifting one's horizon as a result of new conditions and visions, then figuring out how to make progress. It means constantly working to close the gap between what one wants to be and what one is doing now. Like person-hood itself, teaching is a matter of becoming.

Policies that incorporate this recognition of teacher-as-person are the ones most likely to sustain educational improvement. The most effective policies for the improvement of science teaching will be based on knowledge of the nature of classroom teaching, the ways in which it does or does not accord satisfactions for talented people, how it is seen by those contemplat-ing a classroom career (or leaving one), and what qualified teachers who may be attracted by the new plans are actually assigned or expected to do.

Consistent with this view, policies seem slowly to be shifting toward approaches that are neither clearly bottom-up nor top-down. Rather, there is recognition that a balance is necessary between the formulation of gen-eral goals to which most people can subscribe, and the preservation of local and personal capability to develop sensible methods to achieve those goals. To become too prescriptive is to risk transforming teaching into an occu-pation that will attract few people of ability. To become too anarchic is to risk the development of educational programs that do not elicit sufficient support from the general public for high-quality education to occur. But whatever policies are adopted for the improvement of science teaching, the closest attention should be paid to their probable effect on recruitment and retention of the nation's most capable people as teachers. Nothing in the science education policy arena is more important.

PAUL'S STORIES

The many ventures in which I have worked with teachers have all involved attempts to improve their teaching through intervention of an outside agency. Each venture brought out, in its own way, the problematic, even hazardous nature of such enterprises.

Top-Down Innovation

The Nuffield A-Level Physics project, already described in earlier chapters, was a top-down innovation. High points in its development were the con-ferences designed to brief those who were to make the first attempt to teach the course. Our task was both to communicate the intentions so that teach-ers could begin to turn them into their own practice and to generate some enthusiasm, for it was quite clear to all that the trials would involve extra work. That we succeeded was as much a tribute to the love for physics of these teachers, and their commitment to innovative teaching methods, as it was to the quality of our ideas. In summing up the first of these meetings in a closing session, I remarked that the participants were both excited by the new approach and yet terrified because of the work involved together with the risks in trying out innovations in the classroom.

Subsequently, visits to their schools showed that some teachers tried conscientiously to cover every idea we had to offer, even when several were offered as options. Yet one could sympathise. They were naturally unsure, in their first struggles with quite new material, about whether and where they might cut corners. Thus the shortage of time of which the teachers often complained was a sign of a deeper problem: absence of ownership, which led to rigid interpretation. Thus it became clear during the first trials that the teachers would never finish the work planned by us within their school year. Members of the team who had experienced development in other courses advised that this was not a cause for concern. They argued, correctly, that as teachers became accustomed and confident, they would make the work their own and the time problem would ease.

Another key problem was that of disseminating the innovation beyond the teachers of the first trials. I responded to an invitation to speak to a group of physics teachers about the course at a very early stage in our development. An experienced teacher in our team advised me to refuse, but I felt confident that I could convince them of the virtues of our general aims and philosophy. I was wrong. It was an unpleasant experience. The audience were hostile, with their worst suspicions confirmed by my abstract account—here was a university physicist creating new rods for their backs. It was over a year before I dared try again with a similar teacher audience. This time I had the resources for a quite different approach. With equipment on the bench, I led the audience through demonstrations and arguments to illustrate how we envisaged that a particular piece of teaching might be carried out. As relevant instances emerged during this exposition, I highlighted an aim and added it to a developing list. Only after this demonstration and discussion did I talk more broadly about the aims and philosophy of the project. This approach was merely good pedagogy in starting from the concrete and showing the meaning of the abstract by grounding it in the reality of implementation. More fundamentally, it established credibility with teachers, who knew well that the stresses and constraints of classrooms could drown our dreams.

This same lesson was repeated in later years when the course was established and I had to help run the A-level examination described in chapter 5. After each year's examination results had been published, we

met with the teachers involved. The six chief examiners had to spend a day
with up to 200 participants, describing strengths and weaknesses perceived
in the pupils' responses, but also evaluating their own product, the examination questions. These could be tough sessions: Teachers would not hesitate to complain if they thought any part of an examination had been
unfair. They were also very anxious to learn in detail how particular questions, mainly those more open-ended in character, were assigned grades;
they needed such information to prepare their pupils properly. At that time
the actual marking of examinations was a "secret garden," overtly to protect both examiners and the examining body from harassment. As examiners, we stretched, bent, and occasionally broke the rules, first by getting
agreement that marking schemes could be revealed and discussed, then
later by showing examples of real pupil answers in order to illustrate how
they had been marked. With hindsight it seems absurd that such essential
communication had ever been taboo. However, we were also able, at these
meetings, to consult teachers about ideas, ours or theirs, for changing the
framework or procedures in the future, thus supporting a careful evolution.

The Bottom-Up Project

I was made sharply aware of the arguments between top-down and bottom-up approaches about 10 years after the Nuffield physics work when I
joined the steering group of the Secondary Science Curriculum Review
(SSCR), described in chapter 3. A central strategy for this project was to
give modest support to as many local groups of teachers as could be established to pursue their own particular initiatives rather than to follow or
implement any central model. This work was successful in that a thousand
flowers did indeed bloom, with much encouragement and coordination
from a full-time central team. At least some of the stakeholders, the many
groups with an active interest in the science curriculum, were uneasy about
this use of the resources, describing it as the most widespread in-service
course ever designed. Ironically, this would have been seen as praise by the
team. The tangible end products were collections of ideas and materials
advertised as available from the many local innovators. There was also a
very useful set of small booklets on certain key elements for the improvement of school science education. However, the long-term impact of these
seemed meagre in comparison with the scale of the funding.

The contrast with the Nuffield exercise illustrates an important dilemma. Nuffield achieved quite new innovations in curriculum and assessment
and was able to institutionalise them. However, whilst its effect on those
who chose to use the course was clearly profound, many others chose to
ignore it. The SSCR exercise, on the other hand, had no particular product

to point to as its own. The "broad and balanced science" (chapter 3) seemed the most obvious achievement. Yet the review served to stimulate and support a large number of teachers in developing new curricula and pedagogies of their own, thereby raising the status and expertise of the profession.

It would be difficult to produce evaluation evidence to make a convincing case for the long-term benefits of either approach, and even harder to compare them. Such comparison would involve a choice between different assumptions and values in the realm of the professional development of teachers.

Teaching for Professional Development

I learnt more about the professional development of teachers from my teaching the King's College master's degree courses. In my first years in London, M.A. courses for teachers were largely theoretical, justified by the argument that teachers with extensive practical experience could benefit from further academic study. Whilst not disagreeing that this might be valuable, we were stimulated by a newly appointed professor from the United States, David Johnson, to think in a different way.

A modular course grew out of discussions of his idea that we should offer an alternative M.A. course more directly focused on the professional development needs of teachers. Amongst six modules, several chosen from a list of options, a core of "academic" work was maintained, supplemented by studies directly oriented toward classroom work. I taught one module, on teaching styles and classroom interactions. I adopted two roles. One was to deliver accounts of academic work in the field. With a class of about 12 students this could be done in a relaxed and partly interactive way. The other role was to help each of the group to fashion an empirical study of classroom work. As each chose a context in which something of interest was happening in their school, a diverse agenda of issues opened out. Whilst my lectures took half of the time for the first six sessions, the second half of each three-hour evening was spent in discussion, usually about the plans of two of the teachers, with the rest of the group joining in with questions and discussion. The last four sessions were entirely devoted to discussing the teachers' projects. Over the weeks the refinement of each project idea, and the emergence of the data, gave a compelling interest to the classes, whilst the urge to mutual support was also a strong attraction.

I found this exciting. Despite my earlier work on curriculum development, this was my first close encounter with professionals struggling to see their normal work from new perspectives. The quality of the work varied from the good to the outstanding. Some of the final reports were close to the standard needed for refereed research papers. The excitement for me lay partly in the motivation and pleasure of the students as they saw classrooms with a fresh eye, partly in their capacity to pursue a very diverse range of interesting problems, and most of all in the way in which, with my quite modest input from the research literature, they could fashion novel and interesting research results. Of course, these were extraordinary professionals, being volunteers for a course that would mean regular late evenings over the two years required to cover six such modules, with the added requirement of producing full reports on their projects together with extended essays on the lecture part of the course.

I retain from this work enduring impressions of the motivation of many teachers to raise the standard of their work, of the potential for enrichment that lies in their practical knowledge and understanding, and of the ways in which this can be integrated with existing academic studies.

Teachers Responding to Political Innovations

To work on a project that was part of the government's agenda was to take on a quite different relationship with schoolteachers. In the national testing surveys of school science performance for the Assessment of Performance Unit (APU), the schools that had been selected to take part were free to refuse, so the exercise depended on the goodwill of the profession. We started work in September 1978 but felt that we had to talk about our plans at the annual conference of the professional association for science teachers in January 1979. Several hundred crowded into the session. Our presentations were of necessity tentative, rich in background, philosophy, and frameworks, poor in concrete examples. It was an uncomfortable occasion. Much of what we presented, representing first moves lacking the improving disciplines of feedback and trial, could easily be criticised. Some, fearing the longer-term implications of government control of curriculum and testing, expressed their fears in attacks on all aspects of our work. Others, whilst being more sympathetic, found that we could not answer many of the questions that interested them.

At similar presentations two years later, the atmosphere could not have been more different. The key difference was that by then we had some well-formulated questions, and we could produce data giving both overall rates of success and examples drawn from pupils' responses. Teachers wanted to obtain the questions for their own use, partly because we had produced assessments of process aims for which few good examples had been available hitherto. They were also intrigued by the data on pupils' responses. The philosophy and frameworks were accepted both because they now had concrete meaning and because they had delivered some interesting and useful products. Attention was thereby diverted from the fears of government control. We had turned the threatening exercise into one with professional value. But perhaps our original critics were right, for our success in making the policy acceptable could be seen as aiding the construction of the Trojan horse of national control.

Teachers' anxieties about policy depended as much on whether they could identify with its concrete manifestations as with any longer-term view of implications. Indeed, many seemed unaware of the national debates about these implications. Just before the election in 1987 that gave the Conservative government of Mrs. Thatcher its mandate to introduce a national curriculum into the United Kingdom, I had been invited to lecture to a regional conference of science teachers. Near the end of my talk, I displayed a list of statements drawn from the manifestos of the main contesting parties—statements about the desirability of a national curriculum and of national testing. I invited the audience to estimate how many of these were from the manifesto of the outgoing Conservative government, knowing that teachers believed that this type of change was a Conservative idea. When I told them that the statements all came from the manifestos of the *other* two parties, there were gasps of astonishment. This audience had not realised that there was a new political consensus to demand more control and accountability in education. Yet these were committed teachers who had given up part of their weekend to attend a conference about issues in education.

Teachers Involved in Innovations: The OECD Project

A milestone in my thinking about teachers was the international project that Mike and I steered under the aegis of the OECD. In this project, 13 member countries had committed themselves to support collaboration in studying existing innovations in their own countries. The motivation for these countries arose from their common experience that innovations in education rarely achieved the high hopes invested in them. What their policymakers sought was a better understanding of the processes of educational change.

A total of 23 cases, distributed across the fields of science, mathematics, and technology education, were offered for study. A small group of us steered the process, setting initial targets and criteria for the studies, going on to receive interim reports and give feedback about the collection of further data, and ending by gathering full reports from all and distilling the main messages in a book (Black & Atkin, 1996). One of these messages was that over a wide variety of countries and types of innovations, implementation by the teachers was the key to success or failure.

The top-down and bottom-up visions of the reform of learning are sometimes presented as exclusive alternatives, with emphasis on the serious flaws of one or the other. The top-down extreme, in which the teacher is treated as a technician who implements a prespecified plan, fails because teaching cannot be a mere exercise in implementation. The social situations in schools and classrooms are far too complex for such a purely technical approach to work. The flexibility, adaptability, and personal relationships required in the classroom can only be achieved if the teacher can engage both heart and mind in the enterprise.

The bottom-up vision seems to solve this problem by ensuring that teachers have ownership of and commitment to what is to be achieved. But in most cases a group of innovating teachers cannot command the resources or status that they might need to protect their innovation. Notably, they do not have the power to change high-stakes tests.

However, there is more than practicality involved here. The drives for change in education cannot, and arguably should not, all come from teachers themselves. Research might identify ways to enhance learning. School subjects are not frozen entities; they are changing also, so that both the vision of (say) the sciences and the consensus on how they are to be construed as school subjects should also be part of a continuing debate. Moreover, the school's walls have to be permeable, letting the changing needs of society and the needs of their pupils as future citizens have an influence on both aims and methods.

The optimum approach is to be found in the middle ground. An innovation can only work if teachers can personally share, at least in part, in its aims and its motivations; it must evoke some vision or respond to some dissatisfaction that they already feel. Several of the top-down exercises that I have described above were successful only to the extent that such dissatisfaction was already shared by some teachers. They were far from securing universal adoption because many other teachers were not of like mind and could not identify with the visions offered.

Where there is a shared vision, teachers then need support. Innovation is risky: A recurring comment in the OECD study was, "It's pretty scary." So an essential condition in implementing a change is the provision of special support for trials, including help to cushion teachers against failure. Courage and confidence are essential. Confidence produces openness and risk-taking, so it is natural that the best teachers are used for trials. The answer to the main question about an innovation, "Can it be done?," can only be forged in the heat of implementation, where the shape of the innovation may change as it is turned into concrete action.

Wide dissemination is another matter. All of the pressures, such as accountability testing, and supports, such as books, equipment, and in-service training, have to be right. So a systemic approach to reform is essential. But what is also essential is concrete exemplars with which teachers can identify. Such exemplars should be teachers like themselves who have made the innovation work and can respond to their concerns about the details of practicality. Dissemination programmes have to start from where the teachers are in respect to their pedagogy and subject knowledge, and they should be helped to take personal responsibility for their learning, and to develop skill and confidence in implementation, through self- and peer monitoring.

These conditions can be satisfied by innovations that originate from outside the teaching profession, but teachers must become active partners in fashioning them, and be given ample time and support. Where teachers originate innovations, they, too, can meet these criteria, but *the spark of teachers' ideas can only start a small flame, if shielded from premature expectations*. Teachers have to be given status and help from those able to muster the essential systemic support.

To begin any top-down exercise, or to help bottom-up initiatives to expand, there ought to be agencies to which any imaginative group with a plan of good quality can turn. Such agencies have to be able to provide resources and to exercise power over those system constraints that need to be relaxed if the promising plans are to have a fair trial. Sadly, most countries do not have such agencies, and indeed have not progressed beyond the belief that educational reform involves no more than the issuing of edicts with little or no exploration of the practicalities.

Getting It Right

The lessons that I learned in the OECD project were invaluable when a group of us at King's set out to develop formative assessment practices in schools. The research basis for this enterprise has already been described in chapter 6. We wanted to show that the ideas that one could glean from the research could be put into productive practice in the normal routines of classrooms. We hoped then to disseminate tried and tested ideas, involving *teachers themselves* and the examples provided by their work.

Central to our approach was the belief that although the quantitative evidence of the value of formative assessment was clear and convincing, the methods by which teachers could develop formative practices would have to be invented. The research findings did not constitute a recipe. We would have to present the main ideas to a group of teachers, and convince them both that it was up to them to put these into effect, and that in so doing they would transform the ideas into new practical knowledge. At the same time, we wanted to try to understand their processes of change: This would call for fine-grained qualitative study that could capture the classroom complexities, and the interplay for each teacher between the system context, their personal beliefs, and the ways that both they and their pupils perceived and adopted new roles in learning.

With support from the Nuffield Foundation we were able to start work with 24 teachers from six schools. They reacted uncertainly at first. Many were concerned about how they would find the time for this "extra" work. Some did not believe us when we said that we did not have a recipe that would tell them what to do: They thought that we did, and were testing them to see if they could work out the "right answers." However, these turned out to be small obstacles. What mattered was that we provided inputs in ways that made them responsible partners in the research, and that we could also support them, with visits of researchers to observe their classrooms and share ideas with them personally, and with meetings of the whole group where they could share and reflect on their experiences, and derive ideas and encouragement from their colleagues.

For whatever reason, this approach has worked brilliantly. The development of many of the teachers has exceeded our expectations. Through their innovations, we have built up a firm agenda of the components of good formative practice, illuminated by examples of that practice and by teachers' own written and oral accounts. These accounts show that most of them see their participation as a valuable professional development that has changed their classrooms for the better (Black & Harrison, 2001).

This is not the place to describe the details of what has been achieved. The work is still in progress, and has been extended to include a similar development based at Stanford and funded by the American National Science Foundation. Our main tasks now are to understand better how the changes have come about, to develop a theoretical framework to help us understand more clearly the key role of formative assessment in classroom pedagogy, and to design a program of dissemination using our findings and our teacher partners as key resources.

JOINT REFLECTIONS ABOUT TEACHERS

Our experiences as teachers have taught us important lessons. Mature practice can begin only when you cease to worry about your own performance and start to think about whether and how your students are learning. In this perspective, the importance of starting where the learner is—her interests, her present capacity to achieve, her confidence—becomes obvious. The importance of sharing goals, of helping the students to own and be responsible for their own learning, all follow. There is nothing new or remarkable about these lessons. What ought to be emphasized, however, is that just as they apply to the teacher and student, the professor and the undergraduate, so do they apply to the teacher educator and the novice teacher.

The processes of learning to teach are obviously too complex to be condensed in simple formulae, but they must involve internalization of the experiences, during which process they are transformed into shapes and structures that the teacher can use. This is all the more true when they bear on ingrained professional practice, when the purpose of the learning is to change the habitual. Radical change here can verge on the impossible because the practice involved is so demanding and complex that the practitioner has to rely on established routines to survive. An apt metaphor might be the impossibility of learning to ride a bicycle by conscious application of the principles of gyroscopic motion. One obstacle that the profession faces is that many outsiders think the whole process is relatively easy. When outsiders talk of "delivering" the curriculum, they betray their lack of comprehension.

Our Conclusions

One essential that is only recently being realized, albeit slowly and unevenly, is that teachers, like others, need continual opportunities to keep learning. Initial teacher preparation can only be the first step in a regular process, and should be designed as such. Another, related principle is that such continuing education for teachers cannot be conceived solely as transmission of new knowledge and skills. Time and opportunity are needed to step back, to reflect, to consider how new ideas correspond with current practice, to hear from and share with colleagues who work with the same concerns and in similar constraints. If regular opportunities of this kind were common, it would be clearer that teaching is a profession that is taken seriously. Such a norm would be a powerful aid in solving the outstanding problem that ought to confront those responsible for a nation's education, which is how to attract and retain the highest quality of recruits.

Another way to tackle this problem is to have far more thoughtful and careful strategies about change and about accountability. Improvement in classroom learning is a slow and steady enterprise. There can be no quick fixes. Some of the most important changes that might follow from improved policies for continuous professional development would not be dramatic. Many approaches might be used. They might vary. It is unlikely that simple indicators would show that policies were productive, except perhaps that teachers would feel that they were more challenged, yet also more respected and more strongly supported. Whether strategies should be top-down or bottom-up is not the main issue, for when either approach is fashioned sensitively in the light of the need for the professionals to take on new knowledge and also to transform it into practice, the two approaches will converge. Our experience is that many teachers are not resistant to change, but they do resent being treated as robots when their main task is to relate sensitively and helpfully to the development of the young people in their care. A good start in the policy world would be for all who propose change in the classroom to realize this fact. All of those outside the classroom clearly have the right to make demands of teachers and to challenge them about their work. But they also have a duty to understand what their teachers have to do and how they can be supported in doing it better.

8

Some Parting Thoughts

Let's assume that readers patient enough to reach this page have found our tales of science education in the 20th century informative. Let's assume, further, that some of them detect resonance in science education developments during the early years of the new century. The aims of science education are still contested. The role of teachers in determining the curriculum is unresolved. Much external assessment seems counterproductive to student learning. "So what?" as many middle school students are prone to ask when studying some aspect of science whose connection to their present world is not obvious.

We know that lessons drawn from one era are hardly blueprints for solving problems in any other. Context is almost everything. Practical people who shape policy in a classroom, a school board, a governor's office, or a legislative body take action on the basis of what seems not only desirable, but also prudent and timely. Besides, what is desirable in one decade is usually superseded by what is desired in another. The deeds of those who shape a student's education are powered by their underlying values, but they always must act in and on the here and now. They are interested more in principled action than in general principles.

Nevertheless, stories have persisted for millennia as a common human method of passing along understandings from one generation to another. Paradoxically, perhaps, whatever implications they may have for those who come later lie partly in their ambiguity. They must be reinterpreted in the light of new knowledge and experience to make contemporary sense. We have chosen, then, not to try to diminish whatever paradoxes and ambiguities inhere in our stories by trying to clarify, summarize, or distill them any more than we have done already. Rather, we have chosen to highlight them in this final chapter by underscoring a few of the dilemmas that still face the two of us as we try to figure out how to interpret what we have seen and done in the light of the professional choices we have yet to make.

AIMS, BOUNDARIES, AND THE CURRICULUM

The sequence and titles of our seven chapters were developed as we wrote. The trio of curriculum, pedagogy, and assessment would probably emerge in any broad examination of issues in education, so chapters 2, 4, and 5 are a predictable set. What might be a bit unusual is framing the entire volume with a first chapter on aims and the inclusion of chapter 3 on subject matter boundaries. Curriculum debates, it seems to us, gain coherence by examining interplay among curriculum, aims, and boundaries. The evolution of the science curriculum over our 60 years in the field has reflected a tension between advances in our understanding of how students learn and of the process of curriculum design, on the one hand, and, on the other, political initiatives that seek to serve policy ends but with scant attention to these advances. The outcome has been that the fundamental issue—clarifying the purposes of science education in a given period—remains somewhat obscured and therefore as problematic as ever. The discussion of subject boundaries explores a particular dimension of this problem.

The common feature is the need for society to decide how it wants its future to be molded through the education of the young. Perhaps, in societies that are held together by pragmatic compromise rather than by any general agreement about ultimate beliefs, it is too big a question. So the curriculum, mirroring society, is held together by a fragile consensus when it is not being subjected to sharp polarization. While this may be the best that can be achieved, it does mean that the debate about the aims of science education will always be constrained and improvised, for there will be no larger framework of criteria about the development of the young people against which the different positions will be evaluated. It also means that principled debate may always be undermined by a narrower instrumentalism. We may aspire to moral and spiritual development, but we can only engage one another at a more immediate level, such as the presumed needs of a future workforce. Here there is a common language, at least, even if we cannot really fathom one another's assumptions.

One of the underlying beliefs threaded through our several chapters is that education should give young people a capability and a confidence in their own capacity to learn. This is a key element in the interplay between curriculum design and pedagogy, for the design has to create the opportunities for the pedagogy to reach this aim, in particular by transferring responsibility for learning from the teacher to the student. This theme develops further through its evolution in Paul's stories in chapters 5, 6, and 7. A key feature here is that assessment is being transformed from an instrument imposed from outside by a society that wants to grade and sort people to a process that should serve as an intrinsic part of any person's unique development. The new message is that it is through assessment that a person learns to accept and use critical evaluation of his or her own work in order both to improve it and to ultimately develop the essential powers of self-criticism and collaborative evaluation with peers. Such development is not an aim that is peculiar to science education. While it is debatable whether or not science education is particularly well positioned to contribute to it, it seems clear that science education cannot achieve it by working in isolation from the rest of the curriculum.

RESEARCH AND TEACHERS

For two academics whose careers have been framed by the need to work at both teaching and research, it would again seem natural that an account with an autobiographical core should contain our chapters 6 and 7. What has been, and continues to be, problematic for us is how we define ourselves as researchers. In particular, how can we examine our individual histories to acquire perspectives that might help us to evaluate our personal positions more searchingly? There are no right answers, but the main issue for us has been the interplay between scholarship and practice. Our personal involvement both in curriculum development and in the education of teachers has continually kept this issue to the fore, and so has set the tone for our discussion of teachers—rather than of our own teaching—in chapter 7.

The outstanding lesson has been that what is at issue is not smarter design of ideas for teachers to use, or more careful evaluation of the implementation of any innovation by teachers in a trial phase. These are both relevant and important. However, a prior question is the role that teachers might play in actually formulating an innovation and, in the process, generating new practical knowledge. To take teachers seriously as partners would inevitably slow things down and undoubtedly undercut the grand plans and the quick fixes that seem to be advanced regularly to improve educational quality. But those plans are more attentive to political cycles than to an understanding of what it takes to change the teacher's role in the classroom. We are not arguing that there is no useful role for top-down reform. Indeed, the top-down/bottom-up dichotomy is a profound oversimplification. Here again there is no right answer, no set of clear rules to be applied to any problem about how reforms might be designed. Reflections on adequately detailed stories might be the best way to guide choices and action, rather than trying to apply a checklist of explicit rules. If there is one maxim to guide any innovation, our suggestion would be "Make haste slowly." If there were a second, it would be "To remedy weakness, build on strength."

So did we do it right? Any reflection on a career can raise issues of judgment. We are quite unable to muster the detachment to answer the question. Neither can any reader do so on the basis of this book, for our accounts are bound to be partial in exaggerating our importance and in censoring, consciously or unconsciously, unflattering memories.

At a more mundane level, it has been easier than we might have envisaged to parse our personal biographies into the pieces that might best illustrate the themes that constitute the separate chapters of this book. One reason may be that our careers have been diverse. Neither has followed the path of a carefully planned career. A more apt metaphor would be that of wandering around the highways and byways of the territory—and coming by chance and at a late stage of the journey to the encounters with each other that led to this book.

However, the outcomes were not simply random. Our work has been marked by general inclinations (Paul's to be active in changing teaching and examinations while he was also a researcher in physics, Mike's to relate his career in academia to those first seven years in elementary and secondary school classrooms). These predispositions have both put us in the picture when others were considering selections for new assignments and prepared the personal ground for us to make decisions when the occasion arose. This underlies for us the importance that inheres in following, or not, the many unplanned opportunities that arise, small and large. It is said that the devil is in the details. Or maybe it's God. Indeed, both must be involved in what is a steady stream of essentially moral choices. The justification for the approach taken in this book is just this. It is from the detail of our stories rather than in their grander moments that readers might draw profit for their own reflections.

Appendix A

Timeline: Paul Black

1930–1950	Born 1930 in Colombia, brought up in Derbyshire (England) and Rhyl (Wales). Manchester University 1947–1950, B.Sc. degree in Physics.
1950–1956	Cavendish Laboratory, Cambridge—Ph.D student, then junior research fellow in crystallography, 1950–56, Ph.D 1954. Published first physics research paper in 1953.
1956–1960	1956–1974 Lecturer in Physics, University of Birmingham. Research in crystallography and nuclear resonant scattering, teaching several courses and Ph.D students, worked as examiner for school advanced-level physics examinations.
1961–1965	1963 published first paper in education, on physics examinations. 1963–67 Institute of Physics group study on university examinations. 1965–76 Governing Board member of Joint Matriculation Board.
1966–1970	1967–69 Part-time secondment to be joint organizer, Nuffield Advanced Level Physics project. 1970–82 Chief Examiner, Nuffield Advance Level Physics Examination.
1971–1975	1972–76 Higher Education Learning Project (HELP). 1974 promoted professor of physics (science education) at Birmingham.

(continued)

Timeline: Paul Black (continued)

1976–1980	1976 moved from Birmingham to Chair of Science Education and director of Centre for Science and Mathematics Education, Chelsea College, London. 1977 published last physics research paper. 1978–88 Assessment of Performance Unit co-director, school science surveys for government. 1979–82 chair of Education Group of Institute of Physics.
1981–1985	1983–95 series of projects and papers on Technology Education. 1985 merger of Chelsea College with King's College. 1985–90 head of School of Education at King's.
1986–1990	1988–91 Project on Open-ended Experimental Work in secondary science. 1987–88 chair, government Task Group on Assessment and Testing. 1988–92 Primary Science Concepts research leading to Nuffield Curriculum materials. 1989–91 deputy chair, National Curriculum Council. 1990–95 co-chair OECD project (with Mike Atkin) on Innovations in Science, Mathematics, and Technology Education.
1991–1995	1991–93 co-director of research on progression in learning math and science. 1993–98 member of National Academy of Sciences Board on Testing and Assessment. 1995 retirement: become Emeritus Professor at King's.
1996–2000	1996–98 review of formative assessment literature and Inside the Black Box (with Dylan Wiliam). 1998– visiting Professor in Education, Stanford University, California. 1999–2001 formative assessment project with Medway and Oxfordshire schools.
2001–	2000–2 CAPITAL—formative assessment project, King's/Stanford.

Appendix B

Timeline: J Myron Atkin

1927–1943	Born 1927, Brooklyn, New York. Attended New York City public schools. Diploma from Stuyvesant High School, 1943.
1943–1945	Started City College of New York, summer, 1943, Chemistry.
1945–1948	Electronics technician, U.S. Navy, June 1945–July 1946. Returned to City College. B.S. (chemistry), 1947. M.A. (science education), New York University, 1948.
1948–1955	Teacher, high school science (all subjects), Ramaz School (private Jewish day school in Manhattan), 1948–1950. Teacher, elementary school science, all grades, Great Neck, NY, public schools, 1950–1955. Started part-time and summer study for Ph.D. in Science Education, New York University.
1955–1960	Assistant professor, University of Illinois at Urbana-Champaign, 1955. Ph.D., New York University, 1956. Associate Professor, Illinois, 1957. Professor, 1960. First research paper (based on dissertation), 1958. Co-directed first National Science Foundation–supported summer institute for elementary school science, 1959. Fifteen articles, book chapters, monographs, and reports for science teachers, teacher educators, and policymakers.
1960–1967	Initiated and co-directed University of Illinois Astronomy Project, one of the first two curriculum development projects below the high school level supported by NSF. Books for students and teachers published by Harper & Row. First paper on curriculum evaluation, 1963.

(continued)

Timeline: J Myron Atkin (continued)

1968–1979	First trip to England (to observe mathematics teaching in primary schools), 1968. Ford Foundation Travel and Study Award to observe primary school classrooms in England, 1969. Associate dean for research at Illinois, 1968–69. Dean of Education, 1970–79. Director, elementary school science textbook project, Ginn, 1968–1974. Published articles and book chapters, primarily in educational evaluation, teacher education, and education change. Served on advisory boards for several curriculum development projects, the Anglo-American Primary Education Project, and a teacher education project at the Organization for Economic Cooperation and Development (OECD).
1979–1986	Dean of the School of Education, Stanford University, 1979–1986. Ninth Sir John Adams Lecturer, Institute of Education, University of London, 1980 ("Government in the Classroom"). Twelve articles and book chapters on science education, evaluation, and educational change, including three invited articles on education policy for *Dædalus*.
1986–1990	Senior Advisor, Education Directorate, National Science Foundation (full-time position, 1986–87, on leave from Stanford). Evaluator of a national program supported by Carnegie Corporation of New York that linked scientists with public schools, 1987–1991.
1990–2002	Evaluator of science programs that linked universities (Mills College; University of California, San Francisco) with public schools. Co-director of OECD project (with Paul Black) on innovations in science, mathematics, and technology education in 13 countries. Member of several boards and committees of the National Research Council, National Academies of Science, including chair of the Committee on Science Education, K–12 (1999–2002). Principal Investigator, CAPITAL project on assessment in the classroom, a collaborative effort with King's College, London.

References

Anglo-American Primary Education Project. (1972). *Informal schools in Britain today.* Vol. 1, *Curriculum*; Vol. 2, *Organization and administration*; Vol. 3, Teachers and classrooms. New York: Citation Press. (Published simultaneously in Britain by Macmillan Education, Ltd.)

Atkin, J M. (1958). A study of formulating and suggesting tests for hypotheses in elementary school science learning experiences. *Science Education, 42*(5), 414–422.

Atkin, J M. (1963). Some evaluation problems in a course content improvement project. *Journal of Research in Science Teaching, 1,* 129–132.

Atkin, J M. (1966). "Process" and "content" in grade schools (letter). *Science, 151*(3714), 1033.

Atkin, J M. (1968). Research styles in science education. *Journal of Research in Science Teaching, 5*(4), 338–345.

Atkin, J M. (1988). *Education at the National Science Foundation: Some historical considerations and today's challenges.* Stanford, CA: Center for Educational Research at Stanford, Report 88-CERAS-08.

Atkin, J M. (1992). Teaching as research: An essay. *Teaching and Teacher Education, 8*(4), 381–390.

Atkin, J M. (2002). Student autonomy and teacher input. In Robert G. Fuller (Ed.), *A love of discovery: Science education–the second career of Robert Karplus.* New York: Kluwer Academic/Plenum Publishers.

Atkin, J M., & Atkin, A. (1989). Improving science education through local alliances: A report to Carnegie Corporation of New York. Santa Cruz, CA: Network Publications.

Atkin, J M., & Karplus, R. (1962, September). Discovery or invention? *Science Teacher.*

Atkin, J M., & Wyatt, S. P. (1969). *Charting the universe.* New York: Harper & Row.

Atkin, J M., & Wyatt, S. P. (1969). *The universe in motion.* New York: Harper & Row.

Atkin, J M., & Wyatt, S. P. (1969). *Gravitation.* New York: Harper & Row.

Barlex, D., Black, P. J., Harrison, G., & Wise, D. (1995). *Teacher's guide : Nuffield design and technology.* Harlow, UK: Longman.

Black, P. J. (1963, August). Examinations and the teaching of science. *Bulletin of the Institute of Physics and the Physical Society.* 202–203.

Black, P. J. (1986). Integrated or co-ordinated science? *The School Science Review,* 67(241), 669–681.

Black, P. J. (1990). APU science: The past and the future. *School Science Review,* 72(258), 13–28.

Black, P. J. (1991). Technology education in the national curriculum for England and Wales. In M. Hacker, et al. (eds.), *Integrating advanced technology into technology education* (pp. 167–178). Heidelberg: Springer-Verlag (NATO ASI series Vol. F78).

Black, P. J. (1994). Performance assessment and accountability: The experience in England and Wales. *Educational Evaluation and Policy Analysis, 16*(2), 191–203.

Black, P. (1998). *Testing: Friend or foe? Theory and practice of assessment and testing.* London: Falmer Press.

Black, P., & Atkin, J M. (eds.). (1996). *Changing the subject.* London: Routledge.

Black, P. J., Dyson, N. A., & O'Connor, D. A. (1968). Group studies. *Physics Education, 3,* 289–293.

Black, P. J., Evans, D. E., Kimball, W. A., Rutherford, R. J. D., & Whitehand, J. W. T. (1976). The evaluation of university courses—three case studies. *Assessment in Higher Education 2*(1), 46–63. Bath, England: Educational Services Unit, University of Bath.

Black, P. J., Griffith, J. A. R., & Powell, W. B. (1974). Skill sessions. *Physics Education, 9,* 18–22.

Black, P. J., & Harrison, C. (2001). Feedback in questioning and marking: The science teacher's role in formative assessment. *School Science Review, 82*(301), 55–61. *See also* Self- and peer-assessment and taking responsibility: The science student's role in formative assessment. *School Science Review, 83*(302) 43–49.

Black, P. J., & Harrison, G. B. (1985). *In place of confusion: Technology and science in the school curriculum.* London: Nuffield-Chelsea Curriculum. The complete text is available in French in R. Levrat (ed.), (1992) *Technologie: Textes de reference.* Paris, France: Centre International D'Etudes Pedagogiques. Extracts in F. Banks (ed.), (1993) *Teaching technology.* London: Routledge.

Black, P. J., & Ogborn, J. M. (1974). The Nuffield advanced physics course. *Physics Bulletin, 21,* 301–303.

Black, P. J., & Ogborn, J. (1977a). Inter-university collaboration in methods of teaching science. *Studies in Higher Education, 2*(2), 149–159.

Black, P. J., & Ogborn, J. M. (1977b). The Nuffield A-level physics examination. *Physics Education, 12,* 12–16.

Black, P. J., & Ogborn, J. M. (1978). Change and chance. In G. Délacôte (ed.), *Physics teaching in schools* (pp. 3–14). London: Taylor and Francis.

Black, P. J., Osborne, J. F., Meadows, J., & Smith, M. (1992). Young children's (7–11) ideas about light and their development. *International Journal for Science Education*, 15(1), 83–93. *See also* series of Primary Science SPACE reports published by Liverpool University Press 1992–1999.

Black, P. J., Simon, S., Brown, M., & Blondel, E. (1994). Progression in understanding the equilibrium of forces. *Research Papers in Education*, 9(2), 249–280.

Black, P. J., & Wiliam, D. (1998a). Assessment and classroom learning. *Assessment in Education*, 5(1), 7–74.

Black, P. J., & Wiliam, D. (1998b). *Inside the black box: Raising standards through classroom assessment*. London: King's College.

Black, P. J., & Wiliam, D. (1998c). Inside the black box: Raising standards through classroom assessment. *Phi Delta Kappan*, 80(2), 139–148.

Bloom, B. S., Engelhart, M. D., Furst, E. J., Hill, W. H., & Krathwohl, D. R. (1956). *Taxonomy of educational objectives. Handbook 1: Cognitive domain*. New York: David McKay.

Boaler, J. (1997). *Experiencing school mathematics: Teaching styles, sex and setting*. Buckingham, UK: Open University Press.

Bruner, J. (1996). *The process of education*. Cambridge, MA: Harvard University Press. (24th printing; first copyright 1960)

California Department of Education. (1990). *Science framework for California public schools, K–12*. Sacramento, CA: Author.

Department of Education and Science, Central Advisory Council. (1967). *Children and their primary schools. Vol. 1: The report; Vol. 2: research and surveys*. London: Her Majesty's Stationery Office.

D.E.S. (1988). *Task group on assessment and testing—National curriculum: A report*. London: Department of Education and Science.

Dewey, J. (1910). *How we think*. Boston: D.C. Heath & Co.

Dewey, J. (1938). *Experience and education*. New York: Macmillan.

Gagné, R. M. (1966). Elementary science: A new scheme of instruction. *Science*, 151, 49–53.

H.E.L.P. (1977). Higher Education Learning Project (Physics) books (H.E.L.P. London: Heinemann):

> Bliss, J., & Ogborn, J. *Students' reactions to undergraduate science.*
>
> Bridge, W., Elton, L., & Ogborn, J. (eds.). *Individual study in undergraduate science.*
>
> Ogbworn, J. (ed.). Practical work in undergraduate science.
>
> Ogborn, J. (ed.). *Small group teaching in undergraduate science.*

Jennison, B. & Ogborn, J. M. (eds.). (1994). *Wonder and delight—Essays in memory of Eric Rogers*. Bristol and London: Institute of Physics.

Layton, D. (1973). *Science for the people*. London: George Allen and Unwin.

Layton, D. (ed.). (1990). *Innovations in science and technology education: Vol III*. Paris: UNESCO.

Millar, R., & Osborne, J. (eds.). (1998). *Beyond 2000: Science education for the future*. London: King's College London School of Education.

Morland, D. (1994). *Physics: Examinations and assessment.* Nuffield Advanced Science. Harlow: Longman.

Murray, R. (ed.). (1990). *Managing design and technology in the national curriculum.* London: Heinemann Educational.

National Council of Teachers of Mathematics. (1989). *Curriculum and evaluation standards for school mathematics.* Reston, VA: Author.

National Research Council. (1996). *National science education standards.* Washington, DC: National Academy Press.

National Research Council. (2002). *Scientific research in education.* (R.J. Shavelson & L. Towne, eds.). Washington, DC: National Academy Press.

National Society for the Study of Education. (1932). *A program for teaching science*—31st Yearbook, Part 1. (S. Ralph Powers, ed.). Chicago: University of Chicago Press.

National Society for the Study of Education. (1947). *Science Education in American Schools*—46th Yearbook, Part 1. (Victor Noll, ed.). Chicago: University of Chicago Press.

Ogborn, J. (ed.). (1977). *Practical work in undergraduate science* (pp. 119–125). London: Heinemann Educational.

Paechter, C. (2000). *Changing school subjects: Power, gender and curriculum.* Buckingham, UK: Open University Press.

Pellegrino, J., Chudowsky, N., & Glaser, R. (eds.). (2001). *Knowing what students know: The science and design of educational assessment.* Washington D.C.: National Academies Press.

Raizen, S. A., & Britton, E. D. (eds.). (1997). The different worlds of Project 2061. Chapter 2 in *Bold ventures, Vol. 2. Case studies of U.S. innovations in science education.* Dordrecht: Kluwer Academic Publishers.

Rogers, E. (1960). *Physics for the inquiring mind.* Princeton, NJ: Princeton University Press.

Rogosa, D. (1999). *Accuracy of Year-1, Year-2 comparisons using individual percentile rank scores: Classical test theory calculations.* Los Angeles: National Center for Research on Evaluation, Standards, and Student Testing (Report 510), University of California.

Schwab, J. (1969). The practical: A language for curriculum. *School Review, 78*(2), 1–24.

Sheldon, E. A. (1872). *A manual of elementary instruction, for the use of public and private schools and normal classes; containing a graduated course of object lessons for training the senses and developing the faculties of children.* New York: Scribner, Armstrong & Co.

Silverman, C. E. (1970). *Crisis in the classroom: The remaking of American education.* New York: Random House.

Simon, S., Black, P. J., Blondel, E., & Brown, M. (1994). *Forces in balance.* Hatfield, UK: Association for Science Education.

Thatcher, M. (1993). *The Downing Street years* (pp. 594–595). London: Harper Collins.

Tyler, R. (1949). *Basic principles of curriculum and instruction.* Chicago: University of Chicago.

Tyler, R., Gagné, R. M., & Scriven, M. (1967). *Perspectives of curriculum evaluation.* American Educational Research Association Monograph Series on Curriculum Evaluation. Chicago: Rand McNally & Co.

U.S. Department of Education. (1989). *The president's education summit with governors: Joint statement.* Washington, DC: Author.

U.S. Department of Education. (1991). *America 2000: An education strategy.* Washington, D.C.: Author.

Wertheimer, M. (1945). *Productive thinking.* New York: Harper & Brothers.

Index

About the Authors

J Myron Atkin, a professor of education at Stanford University, taught science for seven years in New York elementary and secondary schools. He joined the faculty of the University of Illinois in 1955 and moved to Stanford in 1979. At both universities, he was Dean of Education. He is a National Associate of the National Academy of Sciences, where he was a member of the Mathematical Sciences Education Board, the National Committee on Science Education Standards and Assessment, and chair of the Committee on Science Education K–12. He also served as Senior Advisor to the Education Directorate at NSF in 1986. General research and theoretical interests include improvement of the science curriculum, practical reasoning in teachers and children, and case methods in educational research. In recent years, he has focused on how teachers improve their everyday assessment practices to help students learn science.

Paul Black was a university physicist for the first half of his career. In 1976, his growing involvement in curriculum development and assessment culminated in a move to a professorship in science education. After twenty further years spent directing first a Centre for Science Education and subsequently the Faculty of Education at King's College, London, he retired in 1995. His work in science education has spanned all levels from primary school to undergraduate courses, and has included both curriculum development and research into teaching and learning. In recent years he has served on advisory groups of the USA National Research Council and as visiting professor at Stanford University. His contributions to research and practice in assessment and testing have come to a focus on work on teachers' classroom assessments, which is now having a significant impact on both policy and practice.